SUSTAINABLE HOME

SUSTAINABLE HOME

Practical projects, tips and advice for
maintaining a more eco-friendly household

CHRISTINE LIU

Contents

—

Introduction

—

We are part of the Earth. Beyond the walls of our physical, man-made homes lies a unique environment perfectly suited for our survival, and ultimately our success. From their beginning, humans have utilized all this environment had to offer in order to thrive – revelling in its plenty, and growing strong on its treasures. As our species evolved, we learned to innovate, all in attempts to improve our quality of life.

Revolutions in science and medicine led to industrialization and massive population growth. Sprawling cities emerged, and technologies for dealing with modern life's desires and requirements developed at an alarming rate. Unfortunately, in the process, we lost touch and sight of our natural origins. Our connection with the planet that enabled our rise in the first place grew weaker and weaker, and the result has had devastating consequences on our environment and the creatures we walk the Earth with.

Thankfully, the modern world has started to take notice. The Paris Climate Agreement has unified countries all around the world in combating climate change, and the sustainable lifestyle movement is steadily growing – it is clear that people are deciding that now is the time to act.

The task of caring for the planet may seem a mammoth one, and it's easy to think that the actions of a single person can have little to no impact. However, this is not the case – progressive changes to everyday actions can do your planet and yourself a world of good. So where to start? Well, that's where this book comes in...

Your home is a sacred space. Hopefully a place of comfort, enjoyment, peace and wellbeing. It is within our homes that we build our livelihoods, establish our daily routines, and spend time with loved ones. It's likely that your home is the place you will spend most of your life, even if your 'home' moves from place to place. Our home routines are prime opportunities for sustainable change. This book will take you through the four main rooms of the home – the living room, kitchen, bedroom, and bathroom – and each section includes information, advice and projects for living a more eco-friendly lifestyle. As you read, you'll find that actions in one room can easily be applied to others. The last portion of the book also ventures into basic tips for sustainable living beyond the home – sustainability doesn't have to end on the doorstep.

This book was inspired by my own decision to live simply and sustainably – simply, as I've been on a journey to slow down and live more consciously, but also sustainably, as I find that what is good for our planet is also good for us as individuals. It's taken me a few years to determine what a sustainable lifestyle looks like, but I wanted to curate my best practices into a digestible format that would be meaningful, and hopefully useful. The pictures and thoughts presented in this book are also an extension of my blog, Snapshots of Simplicity, where you can find the latest updates on my journey of living sustainably.

While we are all different, it is my hope that you will find more than a few golden nuggets in this book that will give you the push to get started on your own sustainability journey. For myself, living an eco-conscious lifestyle of greater intentionality and simplicity has led to personal growth and fulfilment in my everyday actions. Although it is a complex journey of continuous learning, investigation, and problem solving, I invite you to join me on this rewarding venture in creating a sustainable home. May the following pictures, words, and thoughts encourage you to be the change you want to see.

Living

—

When you first enter your home, there's a high likelihood that you will walk straight into the living area. It's here that the widest range of activities take place; whether that's relaxing on the couch as you read a book, catching up on the latest television series, or entertaining visitors. Some of the most memorable occasions I've had with family and friends have taken place in our living rooms – it is where we come to gather and socialize.

As an area of the home filled with social activity, the living room is likely to have an array of different types of furniture, decorative pieces, and electronic devices. While we walk through the most common activities and objects associated with the living room, you'll begin to notice that, like in all other rooms in your home, these activities and objects have an associated impact on the planet. For example, there's a good chance that the living room sees the largest use of artificial light – with lamps lighting up your night-time rituals – as well as electronic devices used for your entertainment. Both will contribute significantly to your electricity usage.

Being intentional with how you furnish your living room, reducing clutter, and managing your energy usage are some of the best ways to make the living room more sustainable. You will find that many of these principles apply to other areas in the house, too, which is why this section is placed first in the book. The following pages contain baseline ideas in sustainability practices that you can carry through to all areas of your home.

Minimalism

—

Our world is growing, anticipated to hit a population of 9.8 billion in 2050. While it's great to know that overall human health has improved, at our current consumption rates we will need the equivalent of almost three planets to sustain the future population.

Overconsumption can be attributed to the meteoric rise of consumerism since the Industrial Revolution. Worldwide, our expenditure on household goods and services has quadrupled, going from $5 trillion to $20 trillion in just forty years. Clever marketing convinces consumers that they need the 'latest and greatest' products available; and planned obsolescence – intentionally designing a product with a limited useful life – only perpetuates the problem. It has led to a culture of instant gratification, with companies creating more and more products at greater speed to satisfy consumer demand. As a result, consumers are trapped in a cycle of purchasing lower quality goods that they may not even need, and businesses continue to push for new products, continually extracting raw materials from our earth without considering the planet's resource limits.

Beyond resource depletion, it is estimated that 95 per cent of a product's carbon impact can be attributed to its manufacture (unless it is an electronic device, in which case it uses quite a bit of electricity in its working lifetime too). In addition, for every pound of product generated, seven pounds of waste are produced in the manufacturing process before it even gets to the customer. Most of us have no idea what is going on behind the scenes of the products that we purchase, but knowledge is power – and we can change our habits! The next time you consider a new addition to your living room, such as a game console, a new television, or another piece of furniture, consider all the inputs and waste that product may have caused; from extraction of raw material, to manufacturing and transportation.

Tackling a living space full of items you have accumulated can provide quite a bit of insight into your personal consumption habits, whether it's in the living room, bedroom, or any area of your life. When you take the time to meaningfully declutter, it can help you to better understand what is truly needed in your household, and help you make conscious decisions going forward. We'll explore the basics of minimalist living, which are built upon the processes of decluttering and self-control of future purchases, in an effort to decrease the environmental impact we have as a consumer.

Let's declutter

Begin by taking a look at your space, or a pile of items which may have accumulated in a cupboard or closet. You'll split your belongings into things you want to keep, versus items that don't have much meaning or purpose in your life. To determine what you ought to keep in your home, make sure these things are:

1. Meaningful – perhaps they were gifted to you by a close friend or family member.
2. Useful – a good test of usefulness is to ask yourself whether you've used this item within the last ninety days, or whether you foresee using it anytime soon.

If not, there's a likelihood that you were lured in by an advertisement that convinced you to buy a product without much thought, or perhaps you bought something to use once, but now you never do. You'll find that these items have little sentimental or practical value; most likely, they're collecting dust in a closet or on a shelf.

Instead of simply throwing all of these items into a bin, there are a few ways to responsibly rid yourself of unneeded products that are still in good condition.

If you're looking to give away items in good to near perfect condition, consider:

1. Offering them up to family and friends that live nearby; if someone else can find joy in or a use for your excess items, that's much better than throwing otherwise good products into the waste bin! There is also the added bonus that they will be less likely to buy a new item of their own (which, as mentioned, would add to carbon emissions).

2. Selling; you can do this through online websites such as eBay or Craigslist. Make sure to take clear, well-lit pictures and add a fair sales description to promote both the product and your reliability as a seller. You could also

visit your local consignment, thrift or vintage shops to see if they will buy any of your items off you. Consignment shops typically look for branded, high value items, but you'll be able to sell lower value items online or through secondhand shops.

Perhaps your items look fairly used, or you're simply looking to support a good cause:

3. Donate; charity shops tend to sell used items at fairly low prices for lower income folks that are unable to afford new items. Some charity organizations also use their profits to help fund homeless programmes or provide career training for people with specialized needs.

And finally, for all products that are broken or unfit for repurpose:

4. Recycle; electronics are a product you should definitely recycle. They are often made with precious metals, so for every one million cell phones that are recycled, 35,000 pounds of copper, 772 pounds of silver, 75 pounds of gold, and 33 pounds of palladium can be recovered and reused for future manufacturing. The company from which you bought the product may have a recycling takeback programme, or large electronics shops often have recycling drop off sites. Check all other material and product requirements with your local recycling facility – they should have information on what materials can be recycled. For tough-to-recycle products, I recommend taking the time to reach out to the company that manufactured the product regarding how to recycle it. The more we hold companies accountable for the products they make and where they end up, the more companies will begin to think of more sustainable design options and materials.

Before you buy or receive

After one round of decluttering, it can be tempting to run across another item that you want to buy. However, every time we make a purchase, we are placing a vote – buying a set of neon seat cushions tells the cushion company that customers want more neon seat cushions in the future, and production will continue. So rather than putting your money towards products of little value or utility, which generates greater demand, go through the following steps as a helpful guideline for more conscious consumption habits.

1. Do you need it?
   Before any purchase, ask yourself if you truly need whatever it is you are planning to buy. Will you actually be using it often, or do you only plan on using it sparingly? It is easy to jump towards impulse purchases that you may not actually need, so take a few days to ponder whether or not the purchase is necessary. Leave it in an online shopping cart or on a shopping list for a while before you jump towards the purchase – chances are, you'll forget about ever 'needing' it. You may even have a neighbour or friend you can borrow it from, or perhaps a library of items to borrow at a community centre (tool libraries have popped up throughout the world to allow community members to share electric tools, instead of buying their own).

2. Can you fix it?
   If you're replacing something that's broken, have you had a good go at fixing it first? Visiting a local repair cafe – locally organized meetings where people repair household electrical and mechanical devices – or your nearest repair shop in town could be a more sustainable step, instead of opting for a completely new product that takes more resources and energy to manufacture.

3. Can you buy used?

One person's trash can be another's treasure – buying used is a great idea if you do need to make that purchase. Look for local sources of secondhand goods, or opt for shopping online for used goods in your area. Look for closer sources for these products to help reduce transportation emissions.

4. Can you buy from sustainable businesses?

It is still important to support the businesses that are doing 'the right thing'. If you are able to support a business that is creating new products with sustainable business practices, it's a great way to help generate demand in the market for eco-friendly goods. Look for renewable energy practices at these companies, recyclable materials in the product, end-of-life solutions, longevity and quality. Certifications such as Cradle to Cradle or Fair Trade are some great markers of sustainable products.

5. It's okay to refuse politely.

Regarding gifts and freebies, know that it is okay to say, "no thank you". If your birthday is coming up, let people know your preferences, and be clear with your family and friends that you prefer having fewer things, as part of your effort to reduce your waste and environmental footprint. If others insist on giving you a gift, suggest sustainable and consumable items such as food or bath products. Plants are also wonderful gifts.

We are not defined by our possessions, but our consumerist culture often defines our social status by what we own. Yet, having the newest handbag or electronic device does not make you any better than anyone else, and fundamentally they are only sources of temporary happiness and satisfaction. Consume less, buy better, and spend less time fretting about the latest product trends and more time in personal development, relationships with others, and experiential opportunities.

Energy usage
—

Energy consumption is one of the leading causes of climate change. Though it is caused by various sources, households are responsible for 29 per cent of energy consumed throughout the world, and as a result, contribute to 21 per cent of total CO2 emissions. About 80 per cent of the world's energy is generated from nonrenewable sources, usually fossil fuels such as coal, natural gas, and oil. These fuels were formed after prehistoric plants and animals died and were gradually buried by layers of rock, but the process to mine for fossil fuels is energy and resource intensive. In addition, major environmental harm is attributed to major oil spills, which have an immediate and devastating impact on local wildlife, ecosystems and communities.

The burning of nonrenewable fossil fuels for electricity use also generates greenhouse gases, which are responsible for the greenhouse effect that is increasing our planet's overall temperature. Over the past twenty years, 75 per cent of carbon emissions was generated through the burning of fossil fuels. In addition, these fuels release harmful particulates into the air including sulphur and nitrogen dioxide – both known to damage lung tissue (in both humans and animals) and cause respiratory diseases such as asthma.

A large portion of our current energy consumption is caused by the increase in technology usage in the past ten years. One study concluded that a medium size fridge uses 322 kWh a year, and a mobile phone uses 361 kWh a year – due to background activities such as data streaming and sharing. Our energy usage is an invisible migration from our hands via our phones, tablets and laptops into the digital cloud, so we don't often think of the impact these mobile devices may have. The digital data centres around the world produce a sizeable amount of emissions – estimated to be the same amount as the aviation industry.

As mentioned, data centres are often beyond our reach, and we may not be able to directly influence the energy companies that provide us with power. However, there are a few easy and practical solutions that can make a dent in your energy consumption. Always keep in the back of your mind that as citizens, we must advocate to our leaders, businesses and communities the need for clean, efficient energy sources for a safer planet. Continue to seek ways to optimize on energy efficiency beyond what is written in this book. As you will read later on, your home is just the beginning of your journey towards sustainable change.

Clean energy

The living room relies heavily on energy to power lights and the various electronics and appliances we use for our entertainment. The source of such power is entirely dependent on what is available from our local energy providers, but clean energy sources are not as rare as you might think. It may only take some due diligence and research on your part to uncover options such as wind, solar, geothermal, biomass, and hydropower. None of these sources generate carbon emissions when operated, which is a huge bonus in light of climate change. Nevertheless, they do impact the planet in other ways, so we'll explore each one in turn now so that you might make a more informed decision.

Wind is preferable as an efficient and renewable energy source, as it has the lowest environmental impact on the surrounding area. However, local communities located close to wind turbines have been known to complain about sound and vibration issues, while scientists have observed

some harm to local wildlife. These are rather small issues, and scientists are working to make small improvements to minimize impact, but make sure to research the source of your local wind energy to make a sound judgement.

Solar is another great option, but it often requires more land use – especially for large solar plants located in remote rural areas such as marshlands or agricultural lands. These plants also need cooling technologies that use water – in a water scarce area, it is important to consider the tradeoffs. However, you can also opt to invest in a roof-top solar installation for your own home; a small scale solution that is much more efficient and that has minimal land impact. In regards to the panels themselves, the materials used to manufacture solar panels do emit silicon dust, which poses a risk to manufacturing workers. Toxic chemicals such as gallium arsenide are also used, which must be handled and disposed of properly. It is important to make sure solar

panel manufacturers have a proper disposal and recycling programme at the panels' end of life.

Geothermal energy is found in high temperature areas of land that produce hot water, which is then converted to electricity. The environmental impact is different for each geothermal plant, depending on its production practices. Some produce electricity through closed loop systems that release little to no steam into the air, but others operate with open loop systems that release small amounts of minerals which are drawn from the earth in the process. Sulphur dioxide and mercury are common emissions of open loop systems, and both can lead to acid rainfall.

Biomass – or incineration – captures energy created from burning organic waste material such as agricultural waste and manure, although it raises some concern regarding air quality. Although it may reduce overall waste, it may have a detrimental impact on the air quality of the surrounding area.

Lastly, hydroelectric power is generated through the building of dams, which harness water pressure to create energy. Of course, this can dramatically alter the habitats of aquatic wildlife, lead to flooding, and disturb the balance of ecosystems downstream.

In any case, be sure to understand what renewable energy options are available in your municipality, and look to better understand which options will have the least impact on the environment around you. These renewable energies are no perfect solution and all have some sort of environmental impact, but they are ultimately much more sustainable than nonrenewable fossil fuel alternatives.

LIVING | ENERGY USAGE

Reduce and unplug

The easiest way to improve your energy use is to simply consider all the appliances that are currently turned on. Do they need to be on? Can a space be shared with another individual in your home to optimize the amount of lighting needed? Bring the party and the guests to one room, and keep all the action in the living space so you can keep the rest of the home switched off (it'll save you money, too). If you're streaming data or using the internet, use only when you need to, in order to ease up on the energy needed to power the internet's data centres. Practically speaking, this could mean watching an online video in a lower pixel quality to decrease data usage, or not letting online programmes run when not in use.

When electronics are not in use, especially when you're away from home or out for a longer vacation, unplug them! No need to keep your internet modem, router, lamps, and desktop computers plugged in for a week when no one will be using them. In addition, power cords and chargers that are plugged in without being actively used still draw out energy – also known as vampire energy – which can add 10 per cent to your energy bill. When you include all the homes in the United States, this amounts to about twenty-six average-sized power plants.

Maximizing daylight and sun when and where possible is another easy way to 'unplug' as an alternative to turning on lights. Natural light has many positive benefits too – keeping your home warm during the day, providing light for indoor activities, and reducing mould and bacterial growth. It is also known to keep you happier, more productive, and calm, which is a win-win for both yourself and the planet. You can increase natural light in your home by keeping curtains and blinds open, having light-coloured walls and furniture, or by positioning mirrors opposite windows – not only to give you a quick look at your day's outfit, but also to brighten

the room by reflecting light. Experimenting with how furniture is placed in a room can also help increase the amount of light that enters your window, as it is absorbed and reflected against different surfaces.

When it is time to turn on the lights at night, making the simple switch from a traditional incandescent bulb (500 kg CO2e for 1 year's worth of energy) to a low-energy bulb (90 kg CO2e for 1 year's worth of energy) is a great way to reduce your energy usage – as long as you continue to train yourself to turn off the lights more. If people worldwide switched to energy efficient light bulbs, the world would save $120 billion per year on energy costs!

Reducing your electricity consumption can also be achieved by opting for energy efficient products. When you're in the market for a new lamp, television or stereo, keep an eye out for low-impact products with certifications such as the Energy Star label. These certifications are often backed by government environmental agencies, and provide third party ratings and information on the energy efficiencies of consumer electronics and home appliances. Remember to only buy new when your product is beyond repair though, as manufacturing emissions can negate the reduced carbon impact of a new, 'efficient' appliance.

It takes just a little bit of practice to be become aware of what is and isn't in use, and what you should unplug or switch off. Again, these principles are not only useful for a living space full of electronics, but other rooms throughout the home that house your lamps, spare chargers, and more.

Furniture
—

As mentioned in 'Minimalism' (page 12), our society's consumerist habits have grown tremendously since the Industrial Revolution, leading to resource depletion as well as excess waste. Our relationship with our belongings, such as our furniture, has changed. Decades ago, it was common to invest in a dining set that could be passed down from generation to generation, as furniture was of high value, and made to last. As a family heirloom got passed down it also gained sentimental value for the owner – belongings not only served a function, but also carried memories and stories.

The majority of modern day furniture is manufactured to meet changing trends and offer consumers cheaper prices, instant gratification and often lower quality. Society's attitude towards today's furniture is, as a result, the opposite of the sentimental and caring nature of previous decades. Instead, furniture is seen as disposable – it is quite common to see old mattresses, bed frames, and couches lining residential streets. In fact, 10 million household items are thrown into landfill annually, but nearly 30 per cent of these items could have been reused.

Behind the scenes lies the reality of resource depletion. The timber industry has high demand for rainforest hardwood, a commonly used material in today's furniture, and illegal logging activity occurs in some of the Earth's most precious rainforests. With forests being destroyed at a rate of 1.5 acres per second, it is estimated that approximately 380 animal species are going extinct every day. In addition, it has been suggested that deforestation is the second leading cause of climate change, accountable for 20 per cent of carbon emissions due to the lack of trees available to filter greenhouse gases. Rainforests offer the best conditions to combat rising temperatures, due to their location close to the equator. Of all the trees in the world that can store CO_2 emissions, tropical trees store about 95 per cent.

Let's not forget that the demand for affordable and trendy furniture also affects other resources such as petroleum, raw metals or fabric materials. All these raw materials have an environmental impact and require extensive resources to source, grow, and extract. Instead of opting for new furniture on a regular basis, we can try to apply the principles of conscious consumption (page 16) or even try building our own sustainable furniture as described in the following sections.

Sustainable furnishing

Furnishing your home sustainably begins with a change of mindset. Having a basic understanding of the impact of your furniture on our planet will help you think critically about your next purchase. The following points will serve as a guide to bcoming more environmentally conscious in your furniture consumption. You may notice similar themes of the thought process as seen in 'Minimalism' (page 12).

1. Question why you're making the purchase, and repair or dispose of old pieces responsibly.

   If you'd simply like a new side table or reading chair, think carefully. Give yourself a few days to monitor how you feel without the piece before jumping towards the new purchase, and determine after the end of that time period if you'd be significantly better off with it – only buy what you need. Did a piece of furniture recently break? Consider repairing it through a local repairman or

doing so on your own, unless it is completely unsalvageable. Check your local government or waste facility to determine the proper disposal method for large pieces of furniture.

2. When you decide it's time to make the purchase, consider shopping the secondhand market.

   Used furniture usually comes at an affordable price, and you can often find higher quality at a fraction of the original cost. Vintage or used finds are also a great indicator of the quality of the furniture – the longer the furniture has lasted, the greater potential it has to endure. Scouting out used furniture options can give you a sneak peek into the future condition and quality.

   If buying completely new furniture, support furniture companies with sustainable practices, and remember to invest in higher

quality pieces that can be repaired in the long run. Be on the lookout for responsible sourcing certifications from organizations such as the Forest Stewardship Council (which ensures that all wood is sourced from responsibly managed forests), and check if the furniture is being manufactured or transported with renewable energy. An even better option is to opt for locally sourced furniture that will limit transport emissions.

3. Understand what your furniture is made of and opt for natural materials.

Volatile organic compounds (VOCs), found in many modern day furniture pieces, are chemicals which are offgassed from synthetic solids or liquids. Wood varnishes, chemical coatings, and other synthetic materials should be avoided, as these compounds have been linked to birth defects, endocrine disruption, and cancer. Upholstery made of synthetic fibres, flame retardants, and petrochemical foams have also been under scrutiny as they are in such close contact with our bodies – these chemicals can latch onto air particles and enter our bodies as we breathe. When these pieces of furniture end up in landfill, synthetic particles can enter soils and waterways, and are often too small for water treatment centres to catch.

Cheap plastic furniture, once broken, will not typically be recycled, instead sitting in landfill for hundreds of years. If your furniture already has VOCs or synthetic materials, make sure they are kept in a well-ventilated area, and consider decorating your space with a few indoor plants to help filter the air. Otherwise, if you have the option to buy a new piece of furniture, always opt for natural or reclaimed materials for peace of mind.

Make Your Own: Hairpin Planter

Making your own furniture is another simple and sustainable way to furnish your home (and great fun if you're looking to get crafty). In the following project, I decided to make a simple outdoor planter box with some metal hairpin legs taken from a worn-out side table. These are particularly easy to reuse along with some reclaimed wood to make a table, stand or shelf. The planter box here was also purchased from a local business owner who made products from reclaimed wood that would have otherwise been wasted.

Materials

– 1 set of 4 hairpin legs – the length is dependent on the height you would like your planter to be, or dependent on availability. Be sure to check the weight capacity too
– 1 large planter box or large piece of reclaimed wood
– 12 screws – make sure these are large and deep enough to stay in the wood (number of screws needed may change depending on the legs you use)
– 1 electric drill with drill and screwdriving bits
– Pen/pencil

Method

If building a planter, drill a few holes into the bottom of the box to allow drainage. Attach a medium-sized drill bit to your electric drill, and carefully drill three to four evenly spaced holes into the bottom of the box [2].

Take the hairpin legs and find the holes on the top where the screws will connect. Hold the leg onto the bottom of your wood, and use a pencil or pen to mark where the screws will go [3].

Once marked, place the hairpin legs to one side and using your electric drill, attach a small drill bit to create pilot holes for each of the screw holes. A pilot hole will help the screw go more easily into the wood. Drill a 1 cm (½ inch) depth for each hole.

Repeat this process for each side, aligning the remaining hairpin legs on the bottom of the wood, and marking where the screws should be attached. Drill pilot holes for all the markings.

Switch the drill bit with the appropriate screwdriving bit for the screws. Align one of the hairpin legs over the pilot holes created, and place one of the screws into the pilot hole. Carefully drill the screw into the wood. Repeat until the entire hairpin leg is attached to the wood [4].

Screw all the hairpin legs into the base of the wood with the same method as above. Make sure that all the legs are firmly attached [5].

Now you have your planter, ready to be placed outside on a patio, or if you'd prefer, inside for use as a stylish storage unit.

1

2

3

4

5

Indoor plants

—

Air quality is often thought of as an environmental issue beyond our front door. However, the air quality within our homes is increasingly a cause for concern – the pollutants are not car emissions or fossil fuel-burning factories, but our own furniture and even our homes themselves. Approximately 30 per cent of all new or remodeled buildings have traces of indoor air pollution, as they are often made with synthetic materials to assist with insulation. Buildings with little ventilation have been known to give occupants 'sick building syndrome', a health discomfort caused by over-exposure to synthetic materials. Though the condition may only be temporary and wear off once the occupant leaves the building, long-term issues could arise after long periods of exposure.

As briefly discussed in the 'Furniture' section (page 24), synthetic chemicals can contain volatile organic compounds (VOCs) which release gases that cause long term health issues. Some common VOCs include benzene, which is found in plastics, cleaning solutions, coatings, inks, and oils. Formaldehyde is another common VOC found in pressed wood products, waxed paper, water repellents, or fire retardants, and is classified as carcinogenic.

Multiple studies throughout the world have found that one of the most economical and effective ways to improve indoor air pollution is to keep a few indoor plants. Furnishing your home with plants boasts many health benefits because the plants act as natural air filters. The leaves and roots remove trace levels of toxic vapours, and have also been known to reduce stress, symptoms of ill health, and improve work performance. A recent study in India saw 1,200 plants installed in a twenty-year-old office building. They were surprised to find that their building had the best indoor air quality in the whole of Delhi, and that eye irritation and respiratory problems among employees had dramatically decreased. As a perk, worker productivity also increased by 20 per cent, with the assumption that employees felt healthier living alongside the plants.

As if you needed any, these are all great excuses to start creating your own leafy green sanctuary at home! The following pages contain some information about caring for plants, and a fun terrarium project which, once up and running, requires very little maintenance at all.

Caring for plants

House plants are a beautiful way to decorate your home – whether placed along windowsills, on table tops or on bookshelves. But I think it equally beautiful that they can provide a function: cleaning the air around you and improving your general health. But of course, not all plants are that easy to take care of (particularly if you haven't acquired that green thumb yet).

For those of you who are new to the game, some easy plant species to take care of include:

1. Succulents, such as aloe vera or the snake plant
2. Palms, such as parlour or kentia
3. Cast iron plants
4. Philodendrons

Succulents need very little water but a good amount of sunlight to grow, which is a great option if you tend to forget to water plants.

Be careful not to overwater; less is usually more when it comes to houseplant care.

Once you have collected a few species, take time to understand the specifics of each plant and their preferences; each species will have a different requirement for watering and light, so be sure to read up on best practices. A bright spot or a windowsill without too much direct sunshine is perfect for plants that like a lot of light, such as succulents. For those that need less, the corner of a room or a seat among a selection of other plants and pieces of furniture will do.

Ensure your plant's pot has drainage holes in the bottom, to release any excess water, as well as a tray beneath to catch it. If the tray doesn't dry out relatively quickly, empty it out – excess water will rot the roots of your plant, or encourage mould growth and discolour leaves. If the leaves become dry and brown, and you notice that the soil is quite dry, you are underwatering.

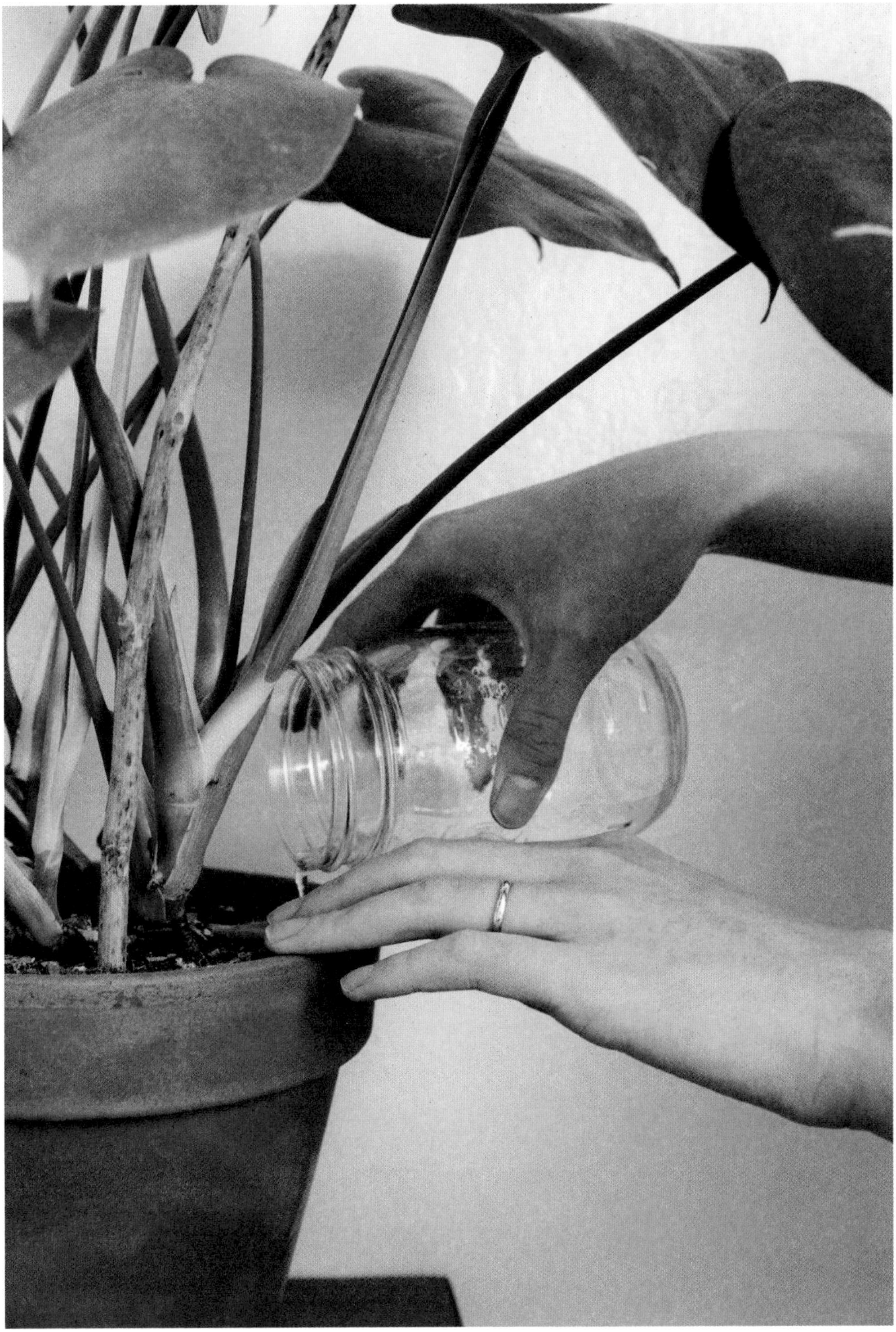

Make Your Own: Terrarium

Terrariums are beautiful, low-maintenance focal points for a living space, and they also make wonderful gifts. They are completely closed-loop systems which are entirely self-sustaining. Soil, plants, and a bit of water are all enclosed within a glass container, and with a little natural light, a greenhouse effect is created. This helps trap heat and moisture, allowing the plants to grow.

Materials

- Large glass container or jar with lid
- Decent amount of small pebbles and activated charcoal – enough to fill the bottom of your glass container up to 2.5 cm (1 inch)
- Potting soil appropriate for your plants – enough to fill the glass container at least halfway
- 2–3 plants of your choice
- Spray bottle with water

Method

First determine what type of terrarium plants you would like to have. Succulents and cacti, which need less water, should be put in a glass container with an open top. Plants that like humidity, such as ferns, mosses, strawberry begonias and calathea are suitable for a closed container. Be sure to buy small specimens.

Take your glass container and fill it 2.5 cm (1 inch) high with small pebbles and activated charcoal. This will help drain excess water and discourage mould growth. The glass container I've used is an upcycled water jug with a small cork in the spout at the bottom to act as a plug [1]. Reuse or repurpose your container if possible!

Place the potting soil on top of the pebbles and charcoal, and fill the terrarium container at least half way [2–3]. Dig small grooves into the soil and carefully position the terrarium plants, ensuring that the roots are covered [4]. Pat the soil down, and spray with a bit of water if it is dry.

Place the lid on top of your terrarium (if applicable for your plant species). A repurposed wooden trivet can be placed over the opening of the container as a lid option, as shown [5].

To take care of the terrarium, place it in indirect light, unless it contains succulents and cacti. You should notice that in the presence of light, the sides of the container will appear foggy and small water droplets will begin to form on the inside (the greenhouse effect). If you begin to notice mould, simply keep the lid open for a period of time to air out the system. If there is little to no fog or water droplets, spray with a little more water.

Kitchen

—

Feeling that rumble in your tummy? It's time to head to the kitchen for a bite! Often the place we go to for a quick refuel throughout the day, the kitchen sometimes becomes much more than that: a place to slow down and focus, taking time and care in preparing feasts and nourishment for friends and family. The kitchen not only helps us to recharge, but also to reconnect. I know mine does.

The food we consume has drastically changed within the past few decades – similar to our consumer habits with products and furniture – and can often have a negative impact on our local communities and ecosystems. Where our food comes from and how it is purchased and disposed of today presents various opportunities for improvement. In addition, the tools we use to prepare our foods and the way we cook and clean can have a direct impact on our bodies and the planet.

As we delve into the kitchen section of this book, you'll find an abundance of recipes and tips for a more sustainable diet and kitchen. There will be plenty of chances to improve your daily kitchen routines in a variety of ways. We easily overlook the true impact of our everyday meals, but a bit of education and awareness can encourage more conscious actions that will transform you, your community, and the way you relate to your food consumption. If more people learn to have a healthier view and value of quality food, we'd have a drastically different world with much healthier people and sustainable food systems.

Sustainable foods

—

Today's agriculture and food industry is capable of producing enough food for every human being on the planet, producing 17 per cent more calories per person compared to thirty years ago despite the growing population. However, the modernization of our farming industry required to meet these demands continues to have lasting and serious negative effects on our environment.

On a factory farm with 35,000 pigs for example, over 4 million pounds of waste will be generated annually – the management and removal of this waste can cause air, soil, and water pollution. The manure may also include growth hormones and heavy metals from animal feed, which can be released into our ecosystems when not properly handled. Heavy machinery contributes to air pollution and due to intensive crop growing processes, industrial farms also heavily contribute to soil erosion. The widespread use of pesticides has caused a massive global decline in bee and other pollinator populations, threatening the future of many fruit and vegetable crops that are dependent on pollinators.

Farms must generate their products quickly and efficiently – much like other consumer industries, which have an increasingly shorter 'time-to-market' cycles – often sacrificing quality for quantity. Studies show that today's food is missing 10–25 per cent of its vitamins and minerals compared to historic, lower-yield equivalents. We all need these nutrients for our bodies to function properly and be healthy, yet our modern day food industry is providing less nutrient-dense, processed foods that in turn force us to eat more in order to meet our nutritional needs.

In the past fifty years, only a certain number of farms were able to meet the demands of the world's industrial food supply. Fewer farms resulted in a much more vast and complex distribution footprint – a typical carrot travels 1,838 miles to reach the dinner table, and about 11 per cent of food's manufacturing emissions come from transportation.

With all this in mind, there is no denying that our relationship and consumption of food needs to change. Large supermarkets, suppliers and our government need to step up. In the meantime, we can vote with our wallets and look for more sustainable, nutritious food options, and be kinder to the planet as well as our bodies.

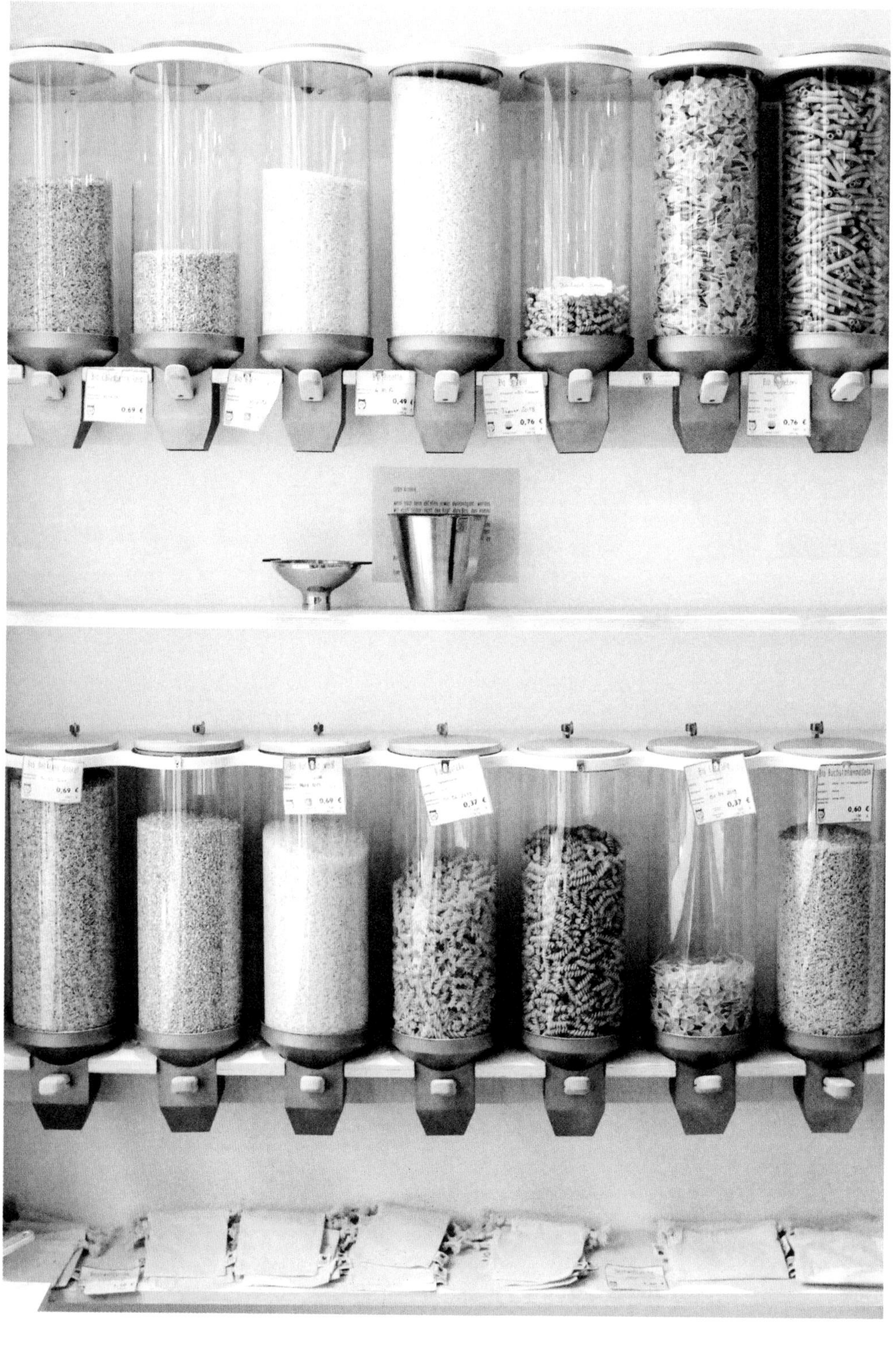

Small scale, sustainable food

The good news is that sustainable food production does exist today – it is often found at a regional level and has much less intensive production practices compared to industrial food production. Local farms produce lower quantities of food that are sufficient to meet the demand of immediate communities, and so are able to focus on growing higher quality, healthier foods. Sustainable farmers also take additional care to seek growing practices that are natural and suitable for their farmland. They are able to use less or no pesticides and chemicals, and avoid common industrial farming practices that degrade the surrounding environment and food's nutritional value.

Choosing organic will ensure that your produce has been grown with reduced greenhouse gas emissions, and only a few natural pesticides, protecting pollinators and benefitting wildlife. Research has shown that organic crops are significantly more nutritious than non-organic, containing more antioxidants.

To find these regional farms, opt to shop at your local farmers market or find a food programme that connects you more closely to your farmer. These local food sources offer fresher options compared to conventional supermarkets, as produce and food is harvested from only a short distance away – and even better, it will taste better! Farmers' markets are typically organized by a public municipality and are held in a public space on a weekly basis. If you're lucky, the farmers' market will last year round, offering a changing variety of seasonal produce. An added bonus is that the vegetables are less likely to be packaged in plastic. Local food services are also emerging, with local farms distributing food boxes to community hubs for pick up on a weekly basis, or offering delivery services right to your front door.

However, not all of us have the luxury of a farmers' market, or access to sustainable food options. If this is the case, understand what is seasonal in your geographical area and opt for those foods at your supermarket. Every type of produce has a peak harvest during the year, when its flavour is at its richest. There is a higher likelihood that seasonal produce is grown naturally, without the need for extra chemical fertilizers or added energy to heat a greenhouse. In contrast, non-seasonal foods are usually flown in from areas with warmer climates, adding not only carbon emissions due to extra logistics, but also raising the price of your grocery bill due to the increased transport cost.

KITCHEN | SUSTAINABLE FOODS

Make Your Own: Food from Food Scraps

Growing small amounts of food in your home is another simple way to reduce your food footprint. Growing a garden comes with quite a few benefits beyond sustainability, but the biggest benefit has been improved health. A study found that preschool children who were almost always served homegrown produce were more than twice as likely to eat five servings of fruits and vegetables a day – and to like them more – than kids who rarely or never ate homegrown produce. Homegrown food is usually much fresher and tastier, so it won't be difficult to pack in your daily nutrients as you enjoy the fresh fruits and flavours of your labour.

A cost-effective and simple way to grow your own food is to grow it from food scraps. This can be done by harvesting seeds before cooking, or saving the stalks of vegetables. For this particular project, lettuce, celery, and spring onions are good candidates, but there are numerous tutorials available online to educate you in growing your own produce from scraps.

Materials
– 1 head of celery
– Knife
– Cutting board
– Small glass jar – wide and shallow enough to fit the base of the celery
– Water

Method
Gather your head of celery, knife and cutting board. Take the stalk of the celery and use the knife to cut it on the cutting board, at least 2–5 cm (1–2 inches) from the bottom of the stalk [1]. Set the cut stalks aside for cooking with or munching on later.

Take the small glass jar, and place the celery in the bottom, cut side up. Add enough water to the jar to submerge the bottom of the stalk [2].

Place the jar by a window and make sure that there is adequate sunlight to allow it to grow [3]. After a few days to a week you will see the inner part of the celery slowly begin to sprout [4].

Once leaves emerge from the base and some roots appear from the bottom of the celery piece, plant the root into soil to allow it to grow to full size.

1

3

2

4

Make Your Own: Herb Garden

A little bit goes a long way when it comes to fresh herbs on a dish. If space is a concern, a small herb garden is another great way to incorporate home-grown food into your everyday routine. The planter box made in the Furniture section of the book (page 28) is a perfect way to house a variety of herbs. Mint, parsley, basil, sage, and rosemary are some low maintenance herbs that are also versatile for all types of cooking.

Materials
- Planter box
- Potting soil
- Variety of herbs to plant
- Water

Method

With the potting soil, fill your pot or planter box until it is 75 per cent full. Make a few dents in the potting soil, enough for each species of herb you wish to plant [1–2].

Take your first herb and gently remove it from its container. If the plant looks root-bound (roots tightly-packed or spiraling around the outside of the soil), tease the roots apart very gently with your fingers. Place the plant into the hole made in the pot or planter box, and cover the base of plant with extra potting soil [3]. Make sure to firm the soil around the base of the plant, to make sure it is secure [4].

Repeat the potting process for the remaining herbs as necessary. Once completed, water each of the herbs so the potting soil feels moist to the touch, but not drenched [5].

When harvesting herbs such as mint, basil, or rosemary leave half of the stems intact to promote healthy growth. Cut parsley stems at the base around the outside of the plant.

In the case of unwelcome pests such as slugs, sprinkle some used coffee grounds onto the soil (a great way to reduce your kitchen waste! Read more on page 56) which can act as a deterrent, and can also be used in small amounts as fertilizer. If you are interested in making your own compost to help your herb or vegetable garden, refer to the composting section on page 64.

Plant-based foods

—

Our demand for meat has doubled per capita worldwide since the 1950s. Unfortunately, this increased appetite has a vast environmental footprint, in more ways than one. Livestock such as cattle, sheep and goats produce methane gas as a byproduct of their digestive process – through belching or manure – contributing to 16 per cent of the world's total methane production. Methane, a greenhouse gas, has a global warming effect twenty-three times that of carbon dioxide.

In the past 250 years, the atmospheric concentrations of methane has increased 150 per cent, primarily due to the agricultural meat industry. If changes are not made to help curb greenhouse gas emissions in the agricultural industry – or any industry for that matter – temperatures are projected to increase a destructive 5.5 degrees Celsius (10 degrees Fahrenheit) over the next century.

Livestock farming also contributes heavily to deforestation and biodiversity loss. Compared to a family that primarily eats grains, legumes, vegetables and fruit, the average western family and its meat-heavy diet would need twenty times more land to produce its food. Rainforests around the world have been destroyed at an alarming rate, either for pasture or for the production of feed for livestock such as soy. Rainforests play a vitally important role, as the Earth's very own air filter. Pesticides used to grow feed, as well as antibiotics used to speed up the growth of livestock have also been known to act as local pollutants, which degrade air, land and water quality.

The standard western meat-based diet requires 4,200 gallons of water per day to produce all the food that will be consumed, whereas a plant-based diet only needs 300 gallons. The UN has acknowledged that water availability is one of our planet's most pressing issues, and will continue to be as we experience additional droughts and water loss alongside the planet's rise in temperature.

Even if you don't feel you can convert to a plant-based diet completely, cutting out meat a few times a week will make a huge impact on your environmental footprint – as well as your health. There are so many delicious, plant-based options available today; you may realize that you don't miss your meaty dishes as much as you thought! So let's dive into some of the alternative options available, which will hopefully tempt you to try making your own nut milk, or get some friends round for some delicious black bean burgers.

Alternative protein sources

The overall footprint of your diet can be cut in half by opting for plant-based foods, which boast not only environmental benefits, but health benefits too. With the number of obese adults on the rise globally – doubling since 1980 – and the number affected by diabetes also quadrupling, medical studies are pointing towards meat and high-fat dairy products as the source. Eating a balanced diet with more fruit, vegetables and alternative proteins can help you avoid the cholesterol and unhealthy fats that come with eating excess animal products. Make sure to stock up some of these healthy options the next time you go grocery shopping, and be on the lookout for even more plant-based options in your local area.

Tofu
Just 110 grams (4 oz) of tofu provides ten grams of protein, as well as a good dose of calcium and iron. It's great baked, mixed into a stir fry, or put into an Asian-inspired soup. Try looking in Asian food stores for freshly made tofu without the plastic packaging.

Lentils
Usually found in curries and stews, lentils are a great go-to for protein. They can be cooked quickly in fifteen to twenty minutes in boiling water. Each 100 grams (3½ oz) is packed with 9 grams of protein, plenty of potassium, vitamin B-6, magnesium, and iron.

Beans
There are many different types of bean, ranging from black, pinto, kidney, or garbanzo. Beans are also packed with protein, magnesium, and iron, and are a great meat substitute for hearty burgers and stews. Swap out a meat-based burger for a scrumptiously seasoned black bean burger, as I do on page 50.

Nuts
Nuts are another great source of healthy fats and proteins. Whether raw or toasted, they work great as a topping for main meals, as an addition to a snack mix, or blended to make a creamy nut milk.

Vegetables
Beyond legumes, remember that other vegetables can also provide a good amount of protein. Kale, corn, peas, and broccoli are a few protein-packed vegetables that are nutrient-dense. Make sure to include more of these for a balanced and energizing plant-based meal.

Make Your Own: Black Bean Burger

Using black beans for your next burger instead of opting for beef is a great way to reduce your carbon footprint. Black beans can be flavoured and combined with other ingredients in many different ways to create a wonderful alternative. Note that you can use lentils, chickpeas, or other legumes as other great substitutes for plant-based patties.

Ingredients

- 60 g (2½ oz) mushrooms
- 1 small onion
- 12 g (½ oz) coriander (cilantro)
- 120 g (4½ oz) canned or cooked black beans
- 1 teaspoon cumin
- 1 teaspoon paprika
- 1 teaspoon garlic powder
- 1 teaspoon salt, plus more to taste
- ½ teaspoon black pepper
- 12 g (½ oz) breadcrumbs, plus additional if needed

Makes 4 servings

Method

Finely chop the mushrooms, onion, and coriander (cilantro) [1–3]. Combine the rest of the ingredients into a large bowl, and use either your hands or a potato masher to manually combine and mash the ingredients together into a sticky mix [4]. You can also use a blender to combine the ingredients, but use the pulse setting, being careful not to blend too much in order to retain the texture. If the mixture doesn't seem firm enough, add additional breadcrumbs to help it stick together.

Form the mix into four large burgers and set them aside on a tray or large plate. Heat a pan with 1–2 tablespoons of oil and once hot, fry your burger [5]. Allow it to cook on a medium heat for at least four minutes on each side, to ensure that the onions and mushrooms are cooked thoroughly. Repeat this process for all remaining burgers.

Once the burgers are cooked, pair with your favourite bun, fresh vegetables, and whatever condiments you'd like [6].

Make Your Own: Cashew Milk

Dairy free milks such as almond or cashew are yummy and healthy options that are really quite easy to make yourself. These milks are great for baking, adding to your morning coffee, or stirring up into a vegan alfredo sauce. A combination of nut milk and coconut milk (commonly found in a recyclable can) can also make for a great ice cream or dairy-free dessert.

Cashew is one of the fattiest nuts and brings out the creamiest flavour, with the added benefit of being cholesterol and saturated-fat-free. The following recipe is one of the easiest nut milks to make at home, with only some water, cashews, sweetener if needed, and a blender.

Ingredients

- 50 g (2 oz) cashews
- 500 ml (16 fl oz) filtered water
- Pinch of salt
- ½ teaspoon of vanilla, or more if needed

Makes 500 ml (16 fl oz) of cashew milk

Method

Before making the cashew milk, I recommend soaking the cashews overnight in water to allow them to soften [1–2]. The next day when you are ready to make the milk, drain he cashews from the soaking water and rinse them.

In a blender, add your soaked cashews, filtered water, salt, and vanilla [3]. Blend for about a minute until smooth, or until no large chunks of cashew remain [4]. There is no need to use a nut bag to strain out the cashew chunks, unless you don't like the texture – keeping the small bits of cashew helps to retain all the nutrients.

Once blended, add additional sweetener or vanilla if preferred. The cashew milk can be stored in a sealed reusable jar or container for up to a week [5].

1

2

3

4

5

Make Your Own: Oat Milk

For those looking for a quick recipe that doesn't require soaking, or for anyone allergic to nuts, oat milk is a wonderful milk alternative. A nut bag is required to filter out the oats, but the solids can easily be reused to start a batter for oat flour pancakes, cookies, or simply adding to your morning oats. Instead of purchasing a nut bag, you can upcycle an old piece of fabric or t-shirt to strain out the milk.

Ingredients
- 53 g (2 oz) oats
- 500 ml (16 fl oz) filtered water

Makes 500 ml (16 fl oz) of oat milk

Method
In a blender, add the oats and filtered water. Blend for about a minute until smooth [1–3].

Set up a nut bag or cheesecloth over a large bowl. Carefully pour the blended liquid into the cloth and use the cloth to separate out all the liquids from the solids [4–5]. Once separated, add additional sweetener or vanilla if preferred. The oat milk can be stored in a sealed reusable jar or container for up to a week [6].

This same method of using a nut bag can be used for any nut milks where larger chunks are left behind, such as almond milk.

Food waste

—

On an annual basis, one third of the world's food is wasted, amounting to 1.3 billion tons of produce valued at 400 billion US dollars. The food wasted in farms, stores and households is enough to feed 870 million hungry people on the planet, posing a serious social problem. However, food wastage includes not only the product itself, but also the time, water, land and human resources used (and wasted) in its production. Food that is produced and left uneaten has an environmental impact encompassing 3.3 billion tons of CO_2 emissions, 250 cubic kilometers of water (3 times the size of Lake Geneva in Switzerland), and 1.4 billion hectares of land. As our planet's resources continue to diminish due to our overconsumption, more countries are pointing towards the reduction of food waste as a preventative measure.

Beyond the emissions needed to grow and ship food products to consumers, their disposal also adds to their emissions. Contrary to popular belief, food and organic waste sent to landfills throughout the world actually has trouble decomposing. Large compacting vehicles fill landfills with as much trash as possible, leaving little room for oxygen or light to interact with the contents. Because of this the organic materials struggle to decompose naturally in an aerobic manner, and instead decompose anaerobically with methane-producing bacteria. Anaerobic decomposition of our organic waste is detrimental when it comes to climate change as it produces methane which is, as previously mentioned regarding cattle production (page 46), twenty-three times more effective than CO_2 at trapping heat in our atmosphere.

In the next sections, you will learn that food waste can be combatted within the grocery shop. Our shops are full of so many foods and delicious options that we often buy more than needed. How we store our food can also help us reduce our waste, since the better stored it is, the more longer it will last. But when food does spoil, there are some methods we will explore to help compost the organic material at home, so you can at least get those nutrients back into your own soil, rather than landfill.

Going shopping

Various regulations in the food industry exist to ensure that food is safe and of good quality, yet some of these standards can be major causes of food waste. One of the most frustrating reasons food is wasted is due to cosmetic flaws. If the product doesn't fit its cookie cutter packaging, or if it has unusual protrusions, colours and scars (otherwise known as organic variations), it is not considered appealing enough and is often thrown away. Supermarkets cultivate pristine displays of fresh, identical-looking produce with little deformities in order to lure in their customers, rejecting 'inferior' specimens altogether. As a result, farmers have started to throw these out straight away.

An encouraging response to this is the 'ugly food' movement, which has been growing in various countries around the world. Local markets and organizations are salvaging food that would otherwise be wasted due to its cosmetic appearance. It is likely that these will be well promoted in your local shop (if it's taking part), but if not, or your local supermarket hasn't quite caught on to the movement, simply consider picking up some single, lonely bananas which may not be considered by the average consumer – it's highly likely these will be left by other customers and subsequently thrown out at the end of the day. It may look peculiar, but it's sure to taste exactly the same. In addition, if you're nearing the end of a farmers' market and notice that vendors are already starting to toss out withering food, offer to take some items that you know you can cook up soon. It's likely they'll sell them to you at reduced price, too.

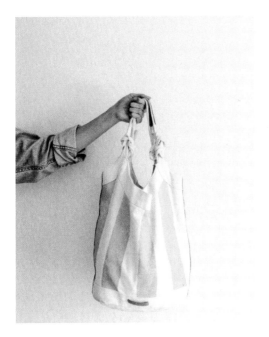

Back at home, it is estimated that families in the UK and US waste approximately 1,500 US dollars in food per year. This could be caused by several factors, including buying too much food, taking 'best by' dates on food packaging too literally, or forgetting to manage leftovers in the fridge. Whatever the reason, there is room for improvement in every household to more efficiently manage your food intake, and reduce the amount that's going into the waste bin.

– Keep in mind how much you purchase, and think critically about your shopping process; only shop for what you need.

– Prioritize eating leftovers before they spoil, and be on the lookout for fresher items in your fridge that are likely to go off more

quickly. For items that have passed their expiry date, the term 'use by' indicates a safety concern (associated with the development of unwanted bacteria, more commonly associated with meat and dairy products), while 'best before' implies that the food is still okay to eat after the date, but just may not taste as great. When in doubt, eat your food quickly, or host an impromptu dinner party so your friends can help you out!

KITCHEN | FOOD WASTE

Tips for storing food

An incredibly simple thing you can do at home to help combat food waste is to properly pack and store your food. Perishable food groups like fruit and vegetables are some of the highest offenders when it comes to wastage, largely because they're so tricky to keep fresh, but taking the following steps can help keep your personal waste to a minimum.

After a trip to the farmers' market or the grocery store, begin to separate your fruits and vegetables. Fruits emit ethylene gas, the ripening agent which causes other produce to spoil more quickly. If your fruits need to ripen further (think avocados, lemons, mangoes, or bananas) just leave them on the side, or bury them in uncooked rice (a handy hack). A container of rice will make the ethylene gas stick around a bit longer, promoting ripenin – working in much the same way that brown paper bags or newspaper wrappings do. And don't worry about spoiling your rice, it will be fine (unless you forget about the fruit altogether!). All other fruits, especially juicy citrus fruits, peaches, berries, and grapes should be left in the fridge, and stored in a dry container with enough space and room to breathe to avoid bruising.

Reusable cotton mesh bags or towels are wonderful to help wick moisture and keep produce dry. Moisture is one of the main spoiling agents, and ventilating your vegetables while keeping them dry is one of the best ways to keep them from spoiling. Mushrooms, for example, should be left loose and dry. Taking off rubber bands and twist ties and rolling up leafy greens loosely in tea towels is also a great way to keep greens fresher and lasting longer.

Carrots, celery, and fresh herbs last twice as long when stored in jars of water in the fridge. Filling the jar full with fresh water and refreshing the water every few days keeps carrots and celery crunchy, and herbs perked up for longer than usual.

Root vegetables such as potatoes, beetroot, onions and garlic can be stored in a dry, cool place with little light. If they are beginning to ripen too quickly or sprout, they can also be placed in the fridge.

If you notice that your fresh foods are beginning to spoil, cooking them right away will help to preserve them, even if you're not ready to eat them just yet. Adding salt and seasonings will naturally reduce the amount of fresh moisture, which is the main cause of spoiling. In general, any cooked foods should be placed in sealed containers to help remove extra oxygen. Having

a range of tupperware sizes, or a variety of bowl sizes and some reusable beeswax wraps (page 74) is particularly helpful. Make sure the seal is as tight as possible with little air flow.

If you are unable to eat all your food at that moment, freezing leftovers in glass jars or metal containers is great – avoid plastic as it can leach into your foods. When packing foods to be frozen in glass, opt for wide mouth jars that have larger openings and not as much of a shoulder. Make sure to not fill the jar all the way to the top – some jars have 'max fill' lines to indicate how full it should be, as foods expand when frozen and could cause your glass jar to break (this is most common with soups and liquids).

KITCHEN | FOOD WASTE

Make Your Own: Sweet Pickled Veggies

If you find yourself with an abundance of fresh vegetables about to go off, then pickling them is a brilliant way to prevent throwing them out – you'll end up with a delicious snack that will last for days (even weeks) to come. The following recipe is inspired by sweet pickled vegetables typically eaten in Asian cuisine as a side dish, something my mother used to make for our family meals.

Ingredients

– Large glass jar with a lid
– 1 cucumber
– 2 carrots
– 1 daikon radish
– Small mixing bowl
– 225 g (8 oz) sugar
– 235 ml (8 fl oz) vinegar
– 235 ml (8 fl oz) water
– Pinch of salt
– Pinch of chilli flakes
  (or any other spice
  you prefer)

Makes one 680 g
(24 oz) jar of pickled
vegetables

Method

Take a large jar – roughly the size of a large jar of mayonnaise – and wash thoroughly.

Take the vegetables, wash and chop into large slices (small enough to fit into your jar of course) [1–2]. Place the vegetables in the jar [3].

Next, mix together the sugar, vinegar, water and seasoning in a small bowl and pour into the jar, ensuring all the vegetables are covered [4–5].

Allow the jar of vegetables to marinate for at least one day in the fridge. The longer the vegetables sit in the brine, the more flavour they will accumulate [6].

These pickled vegetables should be consumed within two weeks, although other pickling recipes that include boiling the vegetables can last even longer.

Enjoy as a side dish to an Asian feast, include it in a spring roll recipe, or try adding a few into your next banh mi sandwich.

1

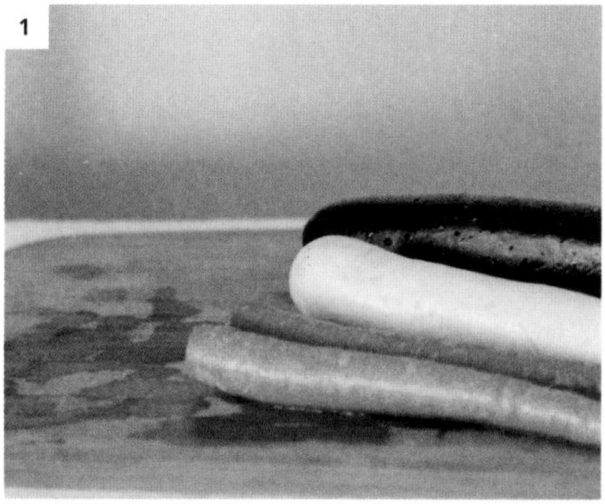

2

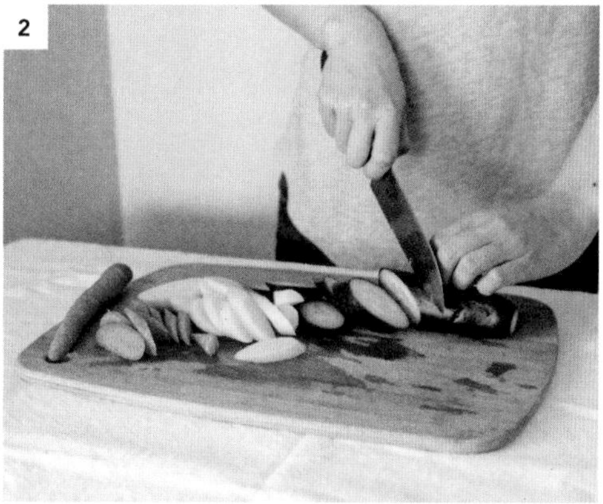

3

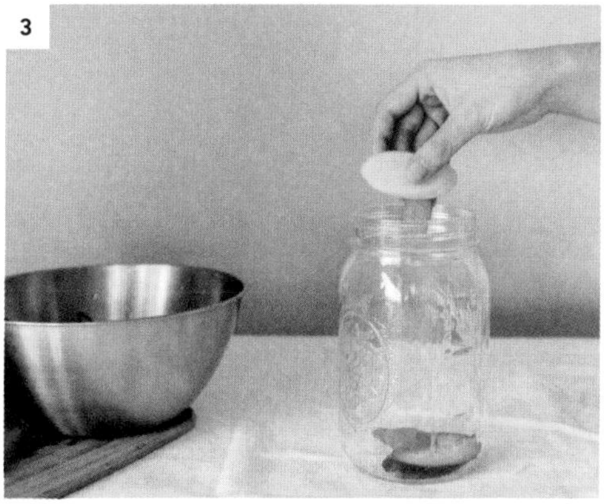

4

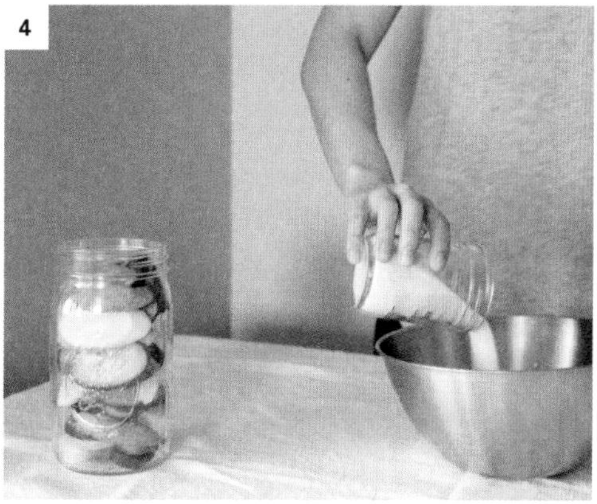

5

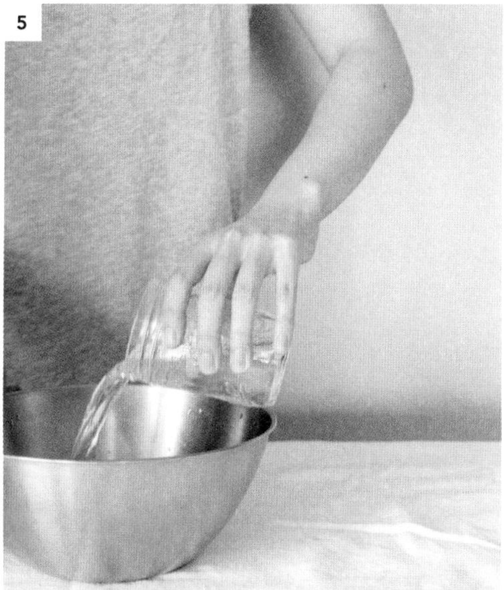

6

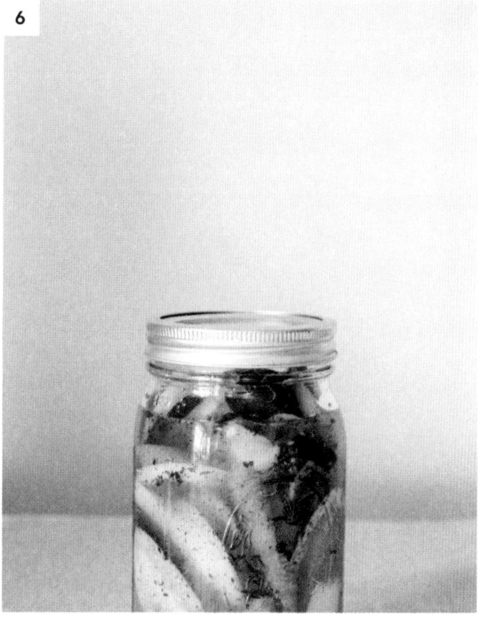

Back garden composting

Instead of sending food scraps to a landfill, where they will decompose anaerobically and produce methane, it is much better to send those nutrients directly back into the earth. Some cities provide council composting bins for its residents, or you may be able to find a local compost drop off site in your local area, such as a farmers' market or community garden. If this isn't an option, there are several ways to compost at home:

– A compost heap/bin in the back garden with leaves and dead plant matter
– A rotating compost bin
– Small dug holes throughout the yard into which you can directly bury natural material

For the simple 'hole-in-the-ground' compost method, all that is needed is a bit of back garden space with open areas of soil. Throughout the day, you can collect scraps including egg shells, banana peel, vegetable scraps and apple cores in a small bin or bowl. It is not advisable to compost dairy or meat products, as this may attract vermin.

Find a small area of soil and begin to dig a hole with a shovel, large enough to hold all the food scraps. Pour the food scraps into the hole once complete and, using the shovel, chop the scraps into smaller pieces. If the soil is a bit dry, pour a bit of water into the hole – using greywater from rinsing dishes is a sustainable way to water non-edible plants and soil (although only if the dishes have been washed with organic, biodegradable detergent). Cover the hole with the dug soil, and the compost should naturally form in a few weeks. Rotate spots throughout your back garden to allow enough time for decomposition.

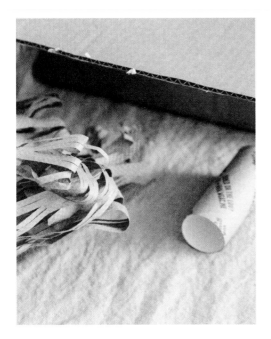

Vermicomposting

For homes with small (or non-existent) yards, vermicomposting, or composting with worms, is a great, scent-free option. The by-product worms produce is also a great fertilizer for gardens and plants. Worm bins can either be purchased online, or made at home. Some bins are made with a tiered system that allows the worms to travel into each tier, effectively maturing the compost in rotation. The simplest form of worm bin (and the easiest to make) is made with two large plastic containers nesting one within the other, with a lid on top. For the plastic container that will be nesting inside, drill a few holes into the bottom to allow any extra liquids to flow out – the bottom container it is sitting in will be there to catch those liquids. There should also be a few holes in the top of the plastic container so that the worms can breathe.

Composting worms are more commonly known as red wiggler worms. You can find these at local bait shops and some gardening centres, or online. These worms will eat their body weight in food and bedding each week and double in population in four months.

In order to make sure the worms have a comfortable home without odours, it is important to keep the bin dark and moist, with 50 per cent bedding and 50 per cent food scraps. Bedding is best made with non-bleached paper products, such as cardboard, brown paper bags, etc. Shred these pieces of paper and let them soak in water for a few hours to remove any rough edges before putting into your worm bin.

Food scraps that are acceptable for worms include egg shells, vegetable peels and scraps, and fruit peels. Avoid meat, grease, fat, bones and dairy. Check the worm bin on a daily basis if possible, to see if the bedding or worm bin is looking a bit dry. If so, use a spray bottle to lightly mist the bedding with water.

Packaging waste

—

Today's grocery shops are commonly filled with products wrapped in packaging. Packaging's primary purpose throughout history was to contain and protect products during transportation, but it has since extended to cater for convenience – customers like to grab pre-prepared meals and snacks on the go, which of course need to be contained in a lightweight, accessible package. As a result, packaging materials have seen advanced technological developments; new synthetic materials and blends such as metallized plastic films (for crisp packets), multi-layered cartons and lightweight packaging solutions were created, all in an effort to more effectively preserve and package foods in a convenient manner.

Yet with the increased use of industrial, plastic packaging came the issue of packaging waste. Ever since the mass production of plastics, there has been an increase in plastic litter as well as a growing mass of non-degradable packaging in landfills. With the lack of end-of-life options for many of these new types of packaging, 91 per cent of plastics today are not recycled, and will either end up forever in a landfill or as litter. Due to the increase of lightweight, flexible plastic packaging, wrappers and bags can be easily swept away by the wind, ending up in wild habitats, forests, or waterways and oceans.

In addition, the chemical processes used to manufacture plastics pose many health concerns. The additives put into plastic polymers in order to achieve certain properties have been found to leach toxins, carcinogens, and endocrine disruptors. Even plastics that are thrown into landfills or littered can leach toxins into local water sources and ecosystems, and if incineration is used as an alternative to landfills, their burning can release even more harmful and toxic fumes into the atmosphere.

Though packaging is not always painted in a positive light, it is actually near and dear to my heart, because I studied it for four years at my undergraduate university. It was during my degree that I became aware of the issue of plastic packaging waste, and began taking steps to decrease my personal packaging consumption a few years ago. This next section contains various tips and best practices for waste free grocery shopping, as well as important information regarding packaging recyclability.

Preparing for a package-free grocery trip

There are several ways to avoid excess packaging in your next grocery haul. Keeping the following items in your bag can prove to be very useful:

– Reusable jars and containers

These can be used at the bulk dry goods section of your local shop (look online to find the one nearest to you). The shop will deduct the weight of your container when purchasing, so be sure to label the lid of the container with the empty weight before you fill up.

Some local butchers, bakeries or deli counters can also place meat, seafood, cheeses, etc. into a container for you. Instead of using several plastic bags, kindly ask the employee to put the product straight into your clean, dry container after weighing.

– Reusable cotton bags and large grocery bags

If your local shop doesn't have a system for deducting the weight of your container, consider using a reusable cotton bag for loose dry goods. Reusable produce bags are great for storing small, loose fruits and vegetables, avoiding the need for the lightweight plastic variety (the kind often ingested by sea creatures such as turtles when they are mistaken for jellyfish). Also don't forget to bring a few reusable grocery bags to carry your other food home! We'll explore a DIY option later on (page 94).

Packaging recyclability

If you need to purchase packaged items, there are a few things to keep in mind. First, opt for bulk quantities of product in recyclable packaging where possible. Packaging products in larger quantities is more efficient in comparison to small, individualized packages. Second, in terms of packaging material, paper, metal, and glass are the best options, but note that these materials have their various environmental impacts (see below). Determine what options are most easily recycled in your locality, and choose materials that are more likely to be recycled than not.

- Paper is natural and compostable, but production can be energy and water intensive.
- Metal boasts easy recyclability in many municipalities, but its extraction requires quite a bit of energy.
- Glass is a great, durable material with accessible recycling options, although it takes quite a lot of energy to recycle due to its high melting temperature.

In some instances, plastic packaging may be unavoidable. Usually all plastic packages or products are labeled with resin identification codes which indicate the type of plastic it is. These identification symbols are triangular arrows with a number in the middle, and can often be found on the bottom of plastic bottles. The following plastic resins are common for most packages and products, some with easier recyclability than others.

- Plastic #1 is polyethylene terephthalate (PET), commonly used to make plastic soda drinks bottles. This is the most common and widely recycled plastic resin.
- Plastic #2 is high-density polyethylene plastic (HDPE), used for heavier products such as laundry detergent packaging, shampoo, or motor oil. This plastic is also widely recycled.
- Plastic #3 is polyvinyl chloride (PVC), used for plastic pipes and medical tubing. PVC is not widely recycled but you can check for local recycling facilities in your area.
- Plastic #4 is low-density polyethylene (LDPE), manufactured for plastic bags and flexible plastic films. LDPE has not been highly recycled previously, but drop off locations at some grocery and retail are becoming more common.
- Plastic #5 polypropylene (PP) is often used for microwavable food packaging, and also plastic caps. This plastic is highly recycled.
- Plastic #6 is polystyrene (PS), often known as Styrofoam. Polystyrene can be found in packaging as a cushioning solution, or for single use cups and food trays. This plastic is not often recycled and will go straight to landfill. However increasing efforts are being made to establish polystyrene recycling centres, so be on the lookout.
- Plastic #7 is any other plastic blend. Some of the plastics included may be compostable plastics such as PLA, or multi-layer plastic film, which is often combined with metals for barrier properties. Due to their blended nature (the materials are difficult to separate) they are not easily recyclable. It doesn't hurt to contact the manufacturer to ask about potential recycling options though.

KITCHEN | PACKAGING WASTE

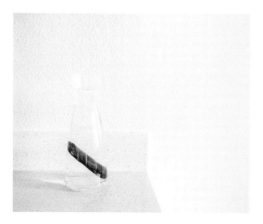 

Plastic free water filtering

Single-use plastic water bottles have become a norm in today's society, owing to the perception that bottled water is cleaner than that from the tap. While this may be true in some areas of the world, most consumers have easy access to tap water that is of the same quality as bottled water – studies have actually found plastic bottling companies using the same source of water used for regular tap water. Armed with marketing schemes that entice consumers into buying 'cleaner' water, companies are able to charge customers 2,000 times more than they would pay for tap water. Producing the current demand for plastic bottles also requires 17 million barrels of oil annually, which is enough energy to fuel one million American cars for a whole year.

To eliminate the demand on petroleum and reduce your plastic wastage levels, find a reusable option. Reusable mugs, cups (often called 'keep-cups'), and bottles are readily available today. If you would like to filter your tap water, an activated charcoal stick is a simple and plastic-free alternative for water filtration.

Traditional water filters today are often produced in disposable plastic cartridges (sometimes recycled by the company). An activated charcoal stick is made from heating wood to an extremely high temperature so that it loses its oxygen content and becomes carbonated. That carbonation acts as a filter and draws out unwanted toxins from your tap water.

Charcoal sticks vary in size depending on the manufacturer. Find a properly sized carafe or water pitcher for your water, place the charcoal stick inside, and let it draw out the toxins for the time specified by the manufacturer. A larger volume of water typically needs more time to filter.

The charcoal stick can be refreshed once a month by boiling it in water for five minutes and letting it dry for twenty minutes before using it again. These plastic-free water filters should last about four months (but check with the manufacturer if in doubt).

Equipment and cooking techniques
—

Over history, cooking over simple wood fires evolved into elaborate home kitchens featuring a host of modern gadgets. Energy and water flow easily through our kitchens as we prepare each meal, yet on a busy day, we can easily overlook the environmental impact of these activities. Take the time to consider the equipment and methods you use to prepare your meals, as they all have impacts on energy and water use. Making small changes to your daily cooking routines can easily help reduce wasted water and resources.

The materials used to make the many gadgets in our kitchen are also of particular concern, especially with the increased use of plastics. Like plastic packaging, plastic dishware or utensils are affected by heat, which causes chemical additives in the plastics to become unstable and to leach into our food. While many of these additives have been banned in certain countries, it is best to avoid plastics when possible, especially in the kitchen where the probability of accidental consumption is higher. In addition, mainstream cookware is often made with non-stick materials like Teflon, which contains carcinogens and toxins known to cause cancer and other health defects. These materials also tend to wear easily, flaking off the pan into your food over time. So once you've made careful sustainable choices with your groceries and are ready to get cooking, doing so with quality equipment made of non-toxic materials is a great choice for the planet and your health; see the next page for more details.

We'll explore sustainable kitchen equipment options to stock up on if you're looking for some new cookware, but will also look into some surprisingly easy opportunities to help reduce our footprint when cooking, washing, or storing food. Whether it is through the appliances we use or how we decide to use them, there are some small steps you can take that have a surprising impact. I've also put one of my favourite one-pot recipes at the end of the chapter, and you'll see why!

Kitchen equipment staples

Stocking our kitchen with the necessary tools and gadgets begins with minimal consumption practices (page 16): only buy what you need. Remember to stop and think before deciding on your next purchase. If you only plan on using something a few times, consider borrowing from a neighbour or friend, and return the favour with a sample of what you may have cooked. Replace kitchen appliances and gadgets only after you've tried to repair them, and if a new purchase must be made, look for energy efficient appliances.

Some great plastic-free options for cookware, which are also long-lasting, include:

1. Cast iron skillets
2. Stainless steel pans
3. Ceramic dishes
4. Wooden cutting boards
5. Stainless steel or wooden cooking utensils

Always check best cleaning or maintenance practices with the manufacturer. For example, cast iron skillets should not be cleaned with soap, just scrubbed and rinsed with water, then oiled when dry to prevent rusting.

At the dinner table, always have a set of reusable dishes, cups, cutlery, and napkins for entertaining family and guests and throwing parties. Though it may appear more convenient to go with disposable options for a party, remember its impact on the environment – petroleum, energy, and emissions are all needed to make the many single-use items that are not typically recycled. If obtaining a large set of reusable dinnerware is expensive, consider visiting a charity shop for some great buys – secondhand dinnerware can be just as good as new.

Glass jars and stainless steel tins are great options for storing food, as mentioned previously. Not taking that food to go and simply storing in the fridge for another day? Consider simply covering a bowl or dish with a plate or pan lid. Cotton beeswax wrap is another great alternative for those who are more accustomed to using plastic cling film, and is completely compostable as it is made from only cotton fabric and beeswax.

Cleaning the kitchen can be done with natural ingredients such as vinegar, water, baking soda and castile soap. Recipes for natural cleaners are included in the Bathroom section on page 102. These cleaners can be paired with biodegradable sponges and scrubbers, or simple homemade rags made from old t-shirts.

Energy and water-efficient practices

Cooking food takes a huge amount of energy. Below are some focus areas for improvement in the preparation of your food.

Ovens have a large carbon footprint in the kitchen due to the energy needed to maintain high temperatures. Limit oven use each week, and make sure to put it to good use with multiple items. Consider roasting some extra veg for use later in the week in a quick lunch. You don't always need to preheat a fan oven either (unless baking bread or cakes) – simply put your food straight in to save energy, and avoid opening the oven door too frequently, as this releases heat. For basic dishes you can also turn your oven off a little early, and leave the door closed, allowing the dish to continue cooking in the residual heat.

When cooking on a gas stove, use the appropriate burner to pot size – make sure flames are not seeping up the sides of the pot to avoid wasted heat. A 15 cm (6 inch) pot on an 20 cm (8 inch) burner wastes 40 per cent of the heat produced. Also take advantage of lids as this will make cooking faster, and more energy efficient as you can cook on a lower heat.

The fridge and freezer are usually the only appliances in the kitchen that run full time, thus using the most energy. If you have a rarely used second fridge, consider unplugging it – you could reduce your carbon emissions by 5,500 to 20,000 pounds a year. For your primary fridge, make sure the temperature is not set too cold, that the doors are sealed tight and not left open too frequently – this

releases the cold air and will require the use of more energy to cool the fridge down again. Keeping a fridge and freezer full of items also helps keeps the atmosphere cold, but try to keep all foods sealed, as uncovered foods will release moisture, causing the compressor to work more. When defrosting items, consider defrosting the night before by placing the frozen item in the fridge instead of letting all the cold air escape into the room.

Water in your kitchen is mainly used in the sink for washing, but also for cooking. When washing produce, wash items in a bowl and save the grey water for watering plants or your garden. When cooking, consider (for example) boiling pasta directly in the sauce with a bit of extra water instead to save water,

and also enhance the flavour. When it's time to clean the dishes, only use the dishwasher when completely full to maximize on water and energy usage, or if cleaning by hand, avoid letting the water run and try to wash and rinse in a sink full of soapy water. Also remember to fix leaks or turn off the tap completely – a sink dripping at one drop per second can waste 1,661 gallons of water in a year.

KITCHEN | EQUIPMENT & COOKING

1

2

3

4

Make Your Own: One Pot Lentil Curry

Now, for my favourite recipe – the reason is three-fold: I love simple, convenient meals which can be cooked in a pot, appreciate how it saves energy, and sincerely enjoy a hot pot of curry on a cold day. This lentil curry recipe is a great fix for a cold winter day when paired with rice, and can be altered with the addition of all different types of vegetables or protein sources. Because lentils cook quickly (within twenty minutes), they are a great plant-based protein choice which can be cooked in the same pan alongside a stew of vegetables.

Ingredients

- 200 g (7 oz) dry lentils
- 1 medium sized onion
- 2 carrots
- 2 medium potatoes
- 100 g (3½ oz) cabbage
- 1 bell pepper
- 1 tablespoon oil
- 1 tablespoon ginger
- 1 tablespoon of curry powder, and more to taste
- 1 teaspoon of salt, and more to taste
- 1 teaspoon black pepper
- 1 teaspoon garlic powder
- 1 teaspoon chilli flakes (optional)
- 2 tablespoons corn, arrowroot or potato starch (optional)
- 235–475 ml (8–16 fl oz) water

Makes 4–5 servings

Method

Begin with rinsing and soaking the lentils in water [1]. Dice the onion into small pieces, before washing and slicing the carrots, potatoes, cabbage, and bell pepper – any vegetable of your choice will work as long as it fits into your pot [2–3].

Place a large pan on the stove over a medium high heat. Once heated, add 1 tablespoon of oil, then add the chopped onion and ginger, and sauté until the onions are translucent. Add the soaked lentils, and any harder vegetables such as carrots and potatoes, which take longer to cook. Add the curry powder, salt, pepper, garlic powder, and chilli flakes, then pour enough water into the pot to cover all the ingredients. Place the lid on and allow to simmer for 10 minutes, stirring occasionally.

Once the lentils and vegetables are almost completely cooked, add the remaining vegetables. Add additional salt to taste, or additional curry powder if you like your dish more spicy. Pour in more water until the vegetables are completely submerged. Allow to simmer for 5–10 more minutes, until all vegetables are softened. Adjust to taste with salt, pepper, and curry powder [4].

If you like a thicker curry, you can add corn, potato or arrowroot starch at this stage. Simply add 2 tablespoons of starch into a small bowl, add 2–3 times more water, and stir to combine until the starch is dissolved. Pour the starch mixture into the curry when it is lightly boiling and stir until the starch mixture is combined. It should only take a few seconds for the sauce to thicken.

Once the vegetables are cooked through, serve with rice or quinoa, and enjoy!

Bedroom

—

Humans spend roughly one third of their lives asleep; something that, if you're lucky enough, you will do in your bedroom. But time is also spent here mentally preparing yourself for the day ahead, and generally relaxing. Bedrooms can be a very personal and sacred space, often a sanctuary from the outside world.

Most of the things we use in the bedroom are as a result quite intimate – our beds and our closets in particular house personal belongings that clothe us and keep us warm. Yet as we continue to explore the changes in our consumption of past decades, the quantity over quality trend can also be found in the fabrics of our clothing, the quality of our mattresses, and more.

Though the bedroom may be one of the smallest areas in your home, there is still plenty of opportunity to make it more sustainable, especially with the turn of the fast fashion industry. The clothing you wear has a footprint – the story of who it was made by, where it came from, and what materials it was produced with. You'll also begin to notice how connected our environment is, as the smallest microfibres in our clothing can end up in our waterways and oceans, and eventually back in our food chain. This chapter will explore and expand upon natural methods to maintain your closet, which, in my opinion, was a truly transformative experience in my sustainability journey – I hope it is as rewarding for you as well!

Closet

—

Clothing production has doubled every year from 2000 to 2014, due to the growth of the fast fashion industry. An estimated 1 kg of fabric puts out an average of 23 kg of greenhouse gases. To top it off, the fashion industry has globalized, so that 90 per cent of all clothing is typically shipped by cargo overseas. It is difficult to calculate the exact impact of the fashion industry's transportation emissions, but there is no denying that the impact is huge – a single cargo ship can produce as much pollutants as 50 million cars in one year.

The raw materials conventionally used in clothing products also have significant environmental consequences. Conventional cotton, for example, makes up 40 per cent of the fashion industry's garments but is water and chemical intensive if not grown organically. With the modernization of plastic polymers, there has also been an increase in the use of synthetic fabrics. In the production of materials like nylon, greenhouse gases including nitrous oxide are released into the air, and can be 300 times more potent than carbon dioxide. Synthetic fibres have also been known to release microfibres in our waterways when washed, eventually entering the aquatic food chain.

From a social sustainability perspective, unfair labour conditions are also a huge concern; numerous clothing companies have been caught cutting costs through inhumane factory conditions and poor payment. The demand for more clothing produced at greater speeds is directly affecting the overall wellbeing and safety of approximately 40 million garment workers globally, 85 per cent of them women. Many remember the story of the 2013 eight-storey garment factory collapse in Bangladesh, which killed more than 1,000 workers and injured hundreds. The collapse was caused by poor construction and working conditions, and a distinct lack of care for employees. Unfortunately, this is one of several instances where garment workers were killed or injured in developing countries due to inhumane working conditions. In response, organizations and certifications such as Fair Trade are working to certify clothing brands to ensure that they are socially and ethically produced.

Clothing is a personal part of our lifestyle, our personalities and makes a statement of who we are. Yet the clothes we select to wear offer multiple ways to become more sustainable. In the following sections, we'll explore some potential areas of improvement in your wardrobe.

Creating a minimalist wardrobe

Curating a smaller set of meaningful, quality clothing pieces can make a wardrobe timeless and practical, and removes the need for heaps of cheaply manufactured clothing. The capsule wardrobe, a concept coined in the 1970s by Susie Faux, embraces the idea of a smaller set of clothes that are versatile enough to wear at a variety of occasions. When looked at from a sustainability perspective, learning to focus your wardrobe on only the pieces you truly need or that you know will last you a longer time will hep reduce your overall closet footprint.

Each piece should be intentionally purchased. Look for quality pieces from sustainable clothing brands if possible, or buy secondhand. Buy less but buy better to support a more socially and environmentally sustainable world.

You can kick-start the process of simplifying your wardrobe by making a list of what you actually need, to ensure that you're making

the most of the clothing you have, and also wearing it on a regular basis. The following is an example list of what a typical capsule wardrobe might include in a woman's closet:

1 formal jacket
1 light jacket
1 thicker jacket/coat
2 dresses
2 sweaters
2 cardigans
3 pairs of trousers
2 pairs of shorts
2 sleeveless tops
3 casual tops
3 button up shirts
2 scarves
4 pairs of shoes

Finalizing the list will take a few trials and errors. Don't worry if you don't get it the first time, because it may take a while to get

used to a smaller wardrobe. But it will be a fun experience learning how to mix and match your favourite pieces into multiple different outfit combinations. If you are struggling and feel like your wardrobe is still lacking, slowly add pieces back into your closet, but intentionally. The idea of this process is not to strip yourself to merely a t-shirt and jeans, but to train your mind to be intentional with your wardrobe and future purchases.

Nailing your personal style is also an important aspect of curating a sustainable wardrobe. While the stereotypical capsule wardrobe will aim for more classic, neutral style clothing pieces, choose pieces that make you feel and look your best. The more you love your wardrobe pieces for how they make you feel, and how they may pair with the rest of your closet, the more likely you will keep it for the long haul. It is important to choose less, but to choose well. You can try to define your style sense through

mood boards or by gathering inspiration from others who have a similar style as you. Pick colours that make you feel your best, or colours that match your skin tone to help compliment your overall look. Also gravitate towards default cuts and pieces that you know will flatter your best assets.

Before throwing away an older piece of clothing with a tear or hole, see if it can be mended or altered. Shoes can also be sent to a local cobbler for simple repairs, extending their life for a few more years. With pieces of clothing that are beyond repair, try to either sell these pieces at a consignment shop, donate them, or recycle if no longer wearable. Several clothing or secondhand shops now offer fabrics recycling, so be sure to check with your local outlet.

Clothing materials

Choosing naturally sourced materials for your clothing will often lead to longer lasting garments, and also helps to decrease the demand for synthetic fabric materials. Polyester, acrylic, and nylon (among others) have been found to shed thousands of plastic microfibres when washed. The materials listed below not only endure, but have significantly less of an impact on local ecosystems.

Wool has been in use for thousands of years. Look for ethically sourced wool from sheep raised in humane conditions. Research shows that adequate living conditions and reduced stress results in less disease and a better quality of wool. Wool can also be found in the form of cashmere, sourced from Kashmir goats and known for its long-lasting, luxurious feel. Remember to store these knits folded in a drawer, not hung up as this may loosen the fabric or stretch it out over time.

Cotton is a staple material for many wardrobes, characterized by its natural breathability and softness. Organically grown cotton doesn't use pesticides and chemicals, often uses less water than conventional cotton, and is softer. Be on the lookout for certifications that promote organic cotton products and fair labour practices. Also avoid poly-cotton blends, which incorporate synthetic polyester fibres, as these blends of synthetic and natural fibres can be more difficult to recycle.

Linen is another natural fibre known for its breathability, made from the flax plant. Linen is a natural insulator, and is valued for its ability to keep cool in the summer months and trap warmth in colder weather. Linen can be more prone to wrinkling, but a quick wash and air dry will remove any wrinkles. The fabric also becomes softer with age and after each wash, making it more comfortable on the skin.

Silk was discovered by the Chinese, and was produced for many years via natural processes.

However, with the increased demand for its luxurious qualities came the addition of chemicals to the production process, and the controversial harming of the silkworms themselves. Vegan silk has emerged as a modern alternative, and is made from silkworm casings only after the moths have emerged and moved on – traditional methods destroy the moth and cocoon in the process. Specific terms such as 'Peace Silk' or 'Ahimsa Silk' will help you identify pieces made using this alternative production process.

Hemp and bamboo are wonderful sources of sustainable fabrics. Their antibacterial properties repel odours that would otherwise remain in other fabrics such as cotton. Both hemp and bamboo are not as resource intensive, and grow quickly without the use of pesticides or chemicals – some predict that hemp will take over cotton production due to its versatility and easy growth. Both hemp and bamboo are beginning to emerge in activewear such as leggings, a great alternative to the synthetic materials most activewear is made from today.

Denim is known for its polluting manufacturing process, which uses heavy metals such as lead, cadmium, and mercury to achieve the blue-hue so many adore. Several companies exist which use more eco-conscious practices, leveraging organic fibres such as organic cotton and plant-based dyes for a more environmentally friendly product, and many established brands are on the lookout for less resource intensive methods of denim production.

Leather, whilst often durable, uses tanning processes which add toxic chemicals. Look for vegetable-tanned leather, responsibly sourced leather without cruel animal practices, or even vegan options – pineapple leather is just one of the examples of sustainable alternatives being explored today!

Resource-efficient and eco-conscious laundering

Some simple changes can be made to lessen the overall impact of laundering, while still keeping your clothes clean. An average household will go through rouhgly 400 loads of laundry each year, using 13,500 gallons of water in the process. It is estimated that 75 per cent of our clothing's carbon impact comes from washing and drying.

Knowing when clothing should actually be washed can help reduce the frequency of laundering, and also increase the lifespan of your beloved clothing pieces:

- All undergarments and activewear should be washed after one wearing, as these pieces are close to the skin and sweat, an ideal spot for bacteria. All other garments that can be worn again should hang in open air to allow the fabric to relax and freshen.
- Tops, t-shirts, and blouses can be washed after a few wears if they don't smell, and sleepwear every two to three wears since we typically sweat more at night.
- Jeans and office wear can be washed after four to five wears, especially if you find yourself sitting in an office for the majority of the day without much physical activity.
- Chunky sweaters and jackets that are not always directly touching the skin can be washed every six wears.
- Remember that delicates such as silks, lighter knits made of cashmere and thinner clothing pieces are good candidates for hand-washing. Though dry cleaning is a common option for delicate clothing, dry cleaning is notorious for using chemicals such as perchloroethylene which has several dangerous health effects, so look for green dry cleaners when possible or handwash if you can, and air dry these delicate pieces.

Once it's time to launder your clothing, make sure that you are able to run a full load. Each household could save 99 pounds of carbon dioxide emissions annually if only full loads of laundry were done. In addition, 90 per cent of the energy used to wash clothing in a traditional washing machine comes simply from heating water, whereas the other 10 comes from running the motor. So when possible, use cold water to wash your clothing – it'll save you money, and increase the overall longevity of your pieces (cold water is much more gentle).

Common laundry detergents on the market today contain synthetic chemicals that are harmful not only to us, but also to aquatic species (once they've made their way into our local water systems). Instead, look for eco-friendly detergents that are phosphate free, biodegradable, and made from plant-based ingredients. You can also make your own washing soda or use soap nuts (berry shells which naturally contain a soap called saponin) as a homemade option, but note that these

homemade solutions are not as suitable if your house has hard water, which is dense in mineral content and more difficult to wash with. If you also use fabric softener, a cup of white vinegar is a great alternative to add during the rinse cycle. Vinegar balances out the pH of total soap and water solution to leave your fabrics softer. There should be no smell as long as it is rinsed properly.

Air-dry all clothing when possible, whether it's with a clothing rack or a DIY string hung up in the backyard. Your household will save 700 pounds of carbon emissions from hand drying your laundry instead of using a drying machine. Direct sunlight can ward off bacteria and also help freshen your clothing. If air drying is not possible, laundering on low heat is best to save energy. Instead of using synthetic dryer sheets to freshen your clothing, you can opt for wool dryer balls as an alternative, and add a few drops of your favourite essential oils to give your clothes a lovely fresh smell.

Repairing and repurposing clothing
—

Cheaply made clothing usually spends only a short amount of time in the consumer's closet. In an effort to follow emerging trends, today's stores are filled with cheap, quickly-manufactured clothes. However, with their sole purpose being to engage with temporary trends, these clothing pieces are rarely made to last. Today, the average consumer is buying 60 per cent more clothing compared to a consumer in the year 2000, but keeping each garment for half as long. There's always a new trend to keep up with, and consumers find themselves getting caught up in the continuous cycle of buying clothing to stay fashionable.

Before long, wear and tear of these cheaply made pieces, along with changing trends, will ensure it is tossed into landfill. In the United States, about 85 per cent of clothing will end up in landfills, amounting to 21 billion pounds of fabric. Even if clothing is donated to a local charity shop, unfortunately only 10 per cent of the clothes are sold. The rest of the clothing is either sent to landfill, or sent off to economically-struggling countries to be sold, drowning out any chance of success for local (more sustainable) clothing businesses.

Similar to the issues behind food waste, fabric waste from the fast fashion industry comes with added implications such as wasted water, resources, emissions and manpower. So the next time you're considering throwing out or donating an older piece of clothing, try repairing or repurposing the fabric first. If the clothing is salvageable with a needle and thread, you'll extend the lifespan of your clothing and make the most of the resources that went into the initial making of it. If you're not so handy with a needle, find your local tailor or repair shop, or ask a friend or family member to help in exchange for help with another task. As a last resort, rip up old garments into rags for cleaning.

In this section, we'll explore some creative ways to either repair or repurpose your clothing pieces in an effort to extend the lifespan of your wardrobe.

Make Your Own: Natural Clothing Dye

One way to reduce clothing wastage is to revive your pieces through re-dying. Most commercial dyes use harmful chemicals and fixatives, which when washed out end up in our waterways. Instead, opt for plant-based materials to dye your clothing. Various plant leaves, roots, peels, or petals can all be used – different plants will give off different colours. Here I've harnessed the juices of soaked black beans from the burger recipe on page 50 as a clever way to restore some colour to my favourite dark clothing.

Materials

- Large bowl
- 2 ltr (70 fl oz) of water (you may need more or less depending on how large your piece of clothing is)
- 200 g (7 oz) dried black beans
- Large cooking pan
- 235 ml (8 fl oz) vinegar

Method

Take a large bowl and fill with 900ml (30 fl oz) of water. Add the black beans and leave to soak overnight [1].

The next day, the beans will have released their colour and the dye will be ready to use. Strain the liquid into a separate bowl and put the beans aside to be cooked separately (see page 50 for the black bean recipe burger which you can use these for).

Next, take a cooking pan and pour in the rest of the water and the vinegar. Place your piece of clothing in the pan, ensuring it is completely submerged, and place the pan on the stove on a medium heat. Bring the solution to a simmer and leave the fabric to soak for one hour – this helps prepare the fabric before it is dyed, allowing the colour to set in [2–3].

Once your clothing has simmered for at least an hour in the vinegar solution, briefly rinse under a cold tap. Empty the water and vinegar from the pot, and replace with the black bean liquid [4]. Place your clothing into the pot and bring to a simmer. The dying process is complete once the colour looks set in the fabric [5]. If you would like a stronger shade, leave the clothing in the dye solution overnight (although be sure to turn the heat off after the first hour).

Once the dying process is complete, rinse the clothing in the sink and wash separately, allowing it to air dry [6]. And there you have it – your new and improved fashion piece.

Make Your Own: Reusable T-shirt Bag

If you happen to have some old t-shirts or sheets that are no longer used, consider upcycling them into some functional items for the household. Old pillowcases and sheets can be sewn to make cloth produce bags, and old t-shirts can be converted into yarn to be crocheted. Old fabrics can also be turned into simple dish rags or even a cloth nut bag for making nut milks. Sewing the edges of the fabric can also prevent curling, and give it a cleaner look. In this project, I convert a t-shirt into a reusable bag using just a pair of scissors.

Materials
– 1 t-shirt
– 1 pair of scissors

Method

Have the shirt turned up on the side you would like to have facing inwards – you will be flipping the bag inside out for the final step.

Lay the t-shirt flat on a table or flat surface. Cut both of the t-shirt's sleeves off, so you end up with a tank top [1].

Cut a deep U shape from the neckline to create the handles of the bag. You can compare how deep the U shape should be by placing another reusable bag on top of the t-shirt [2–4].

At the base of the t-shirt, cut strips at least 2 inches long perpendicular to the bottom of the shirt [5]. These should come to resemble tassels [6]. Be sure to cut upwards along the edges of the far left and right tassels, to separate them.

Moving from left to right, tie the top and bottom matching tassel into a knot. Continue to go across the bottom of the t-shirt, tying a single knot with each top and bottom matching tassel. To secure these knots, go back to the left side of the shirt. Take the top tassel from the first knot, and tie that tassel with the bottom tassel of the knot to the right of it. Continue this process, tying the left top tassel with the right bottom tassel of each existing knot throughout the length of the base.

Once all the knots are tied, tie the first and last knots once more. Flip the bag inside out, and you will notice that a seam has been formed [7]. Your bag is now complete and ready to be filled with groceries or produce from your next farmers market trip [8].

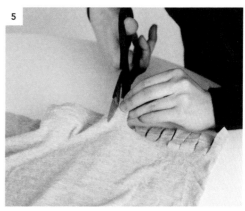

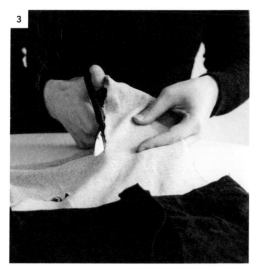

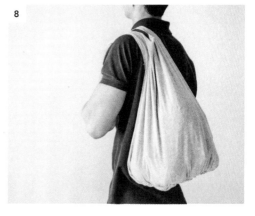

Sleep

—

Humans spend a third of their lives sleeping. It is during this time of rest that our bodies go through important biological processes to repair themselves, such as balancing hormone levels and strengthening our immune system. If these hours of rest are not productive, our body is unable to function properly or efficiently throughout the day, affecting our ability to make sound decisions or be able to put full energy into our daytime activities. Your quality of sleep affects your own personal sustainability!

Yet as our bodies are repairing themselves each night, they are also exposed to your bedroom's environment for a long period of time. The air we breathe and surfaces our skin touches all can have a direct affect on our bodies. Similar to our other household furniture (page 24), the items in our bedrooms can emit harmful fumes when made out of synthetic materials and chemicals, and these pieces can end up in our environment once thrown away. It is important to consider natural solutions for our bedrooms when we spend so much vital, restorative time in that space.

The following sections will look into some things to consider when it comes to furnishing your bed, such as materials to avoid when it comes to your mattress, sheets, and pillows. We'll also reinforce conscious consumption principles (page 16) in this chapter, assessing the quality of modern mattresses available on the market, and focusing on what properties to look out for.

Lastly, I've created a simple recipe for a room spray to provide a more restful ambiance as you drift off into a quality night's sleep – it reminds me of yoga studios right before I head off to a peaceful savasana, and I hope you find it as soothing as I do.

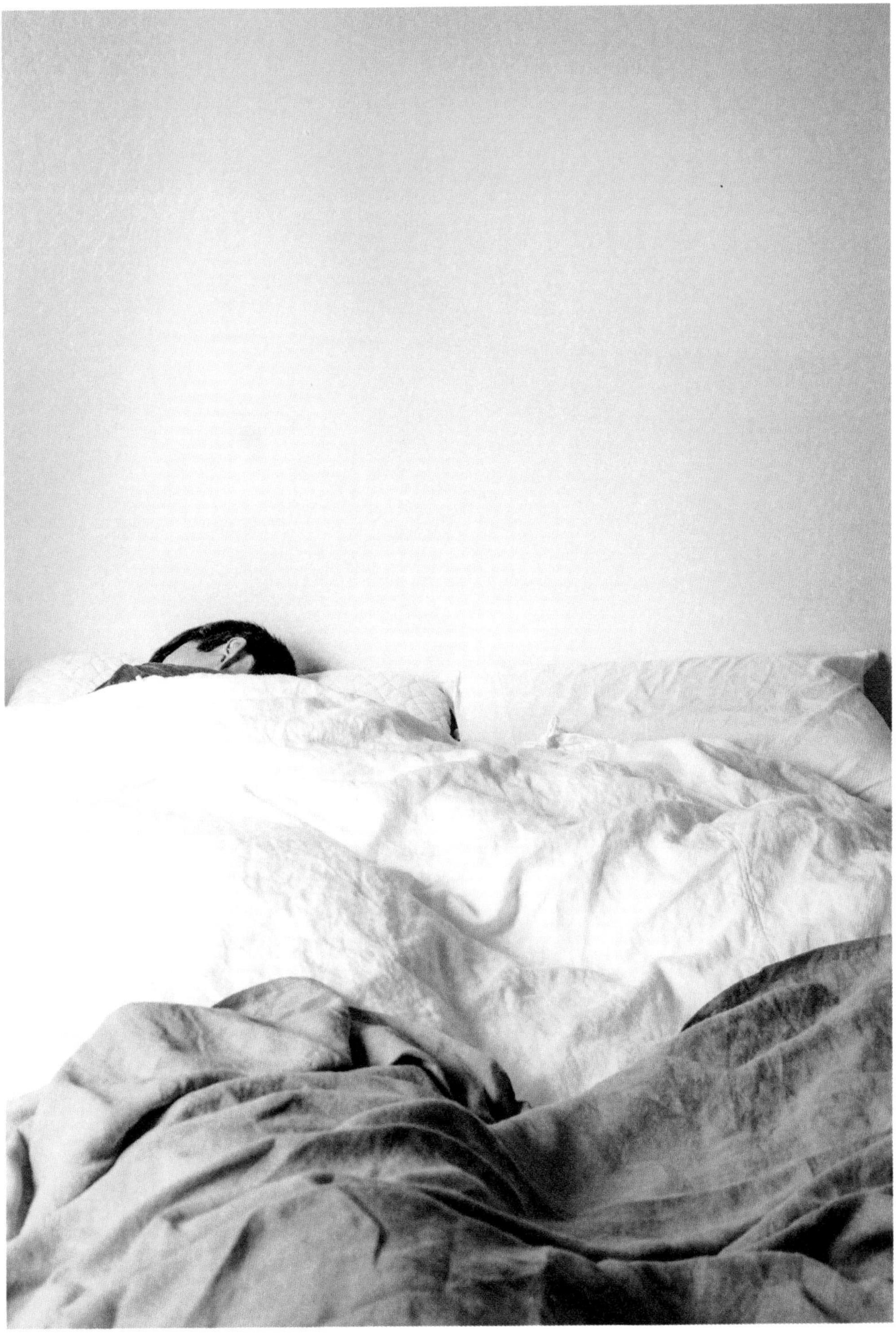

Furniture

Most modern mattresses are built cheaply and not made to last – millions of mattresses are tossed into landfills each year, and due to their bulky nature, take up a huge amount of resources in transportation. Salvaging the foam, metal and wood material from mattresses can divert thousands of tons of waste, but this doesn't always happen, as proper disposal of mattresses can be expensive if local waste facilities charge.

Although expensive initially, buying a good-quality, sustainable mattress can help reduce the demand for the synthetic materials used to make most mattresses today. In addition, recent studies have found that flame retardants, petrochemicals and other synthetic materials commonly found in mattresses and sofas are causing major health concerns. For example, many mattresses are made with polyurethane foam, a nonrenewable plastic which has been found to cause lung complications, skin irritation, and swelling in the brain – not the most pleasant scenario when you want a good night's rest!

Mattresses are a long-term investment, and it is best to use the one you already own until it is ready to be donated. If you are concerned about the chemicals, find a safe cover to put over the mattress to avoid inhaling the fumes, keep the windows open when possible and have a few indoor plants to help filter the air. However, if you are out to look for a new, sustainable option, seek out mattresses with natural latex materials, organic cotton, and wool. Check mattress manufacturers and their sustainability practices, and buy a mattress that will last you a lifetime. Natural, quality materials are likely to keep a mattress intact for twice the average lifespan of a synthetic material mattress. You might also consider a minimalist Japanese-style futon made from all natural materials – these use less material than a common mattress with box springs.

Similar to clothing materials, mattresses should be covered with natural fabrics. Cotton sheets work great for breathability, whereas wool blankets can keep you warm in cold weather – all contributing to a great night's sleep.

Make Your Own: Room Spray

Set your bedroom's ambiance with a refreshing and calming scented spray and help improve your night's sleep. I love the smell of lavender and tea tree essential oils when practising yoga, and often use these same oils to help me relax before sleeping. This simple room spray works wonders for a good night's rest.

Materials
– Bowl
– 100ml (3½ fl oz) filtered water
– Spray bottle
– Essential oil of your choice
– 1 tablespoon witch hazel or vodka

Method
Placing a bowl underneath to catch spills, pour the water into your spray bottle [2]. Add 10 drops of essential oil to the water, along with the 1 tablespoon of witch hazel or vodka – this will help combine the water and oils [3–4].

Give the bottle a good shake (with the lid on), then spray once – if the scent is too weak for your liking, add a few more drops of your desired essential oil [5] .

This spray can be used to freshen up your closet, your bedroom before you sleep, or any other room in your home [6].

1

2

3

4
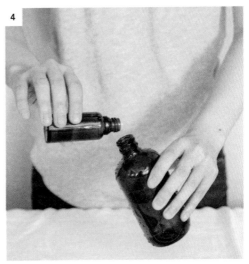

5

6

Bathroom

—

Scrub, wash, rinse and repeat. The bathroom gives us a space to cleanse our bodies before the day begins and when it is over. We utilize a plethora of personal care products and plenty of water to take care of ourselves on a routine basis – there's no denying that the bathroom can be filled with many small rituals to help you feel your best.

Nevertheless, the many products we use in the consumer body care industry today often contain questionable ingredients – some carcinogenic. The alluring scents and attractive textures of these products are created using harmful chemicals. The way we handle water usage in the bathroom is also key when it comes to sustainability, as many of us take for granted the water that flows so smoothly from the tap, toilet and bathtub.

There are numerous opportunities in the bathroom to use natural ingredients and to use recipes to make our own everyday body products – tooth, body, and haircare products can all be simply made, as you'll see in the examples that follow. Not only will your body thank you for using natural body products, but the planet will too. You will also find some simple ways to reduce your water consumption – aside from the garden (if you have one) the bathroom is the primary area of water usage in most households.

Toothcare

—

Today's dental industry offers a plethora of products to choose from – whitening solutions, products to combat gum disease... the possibilities are almost endless. With an overwhelming amount of products, it can be easy to stock up on a variety of options to help maintain those pearly whites. There's no denying the power of a beautiful smile and of course, healthy teeth to help you eat delicious foods everyday!

Brands market their complex products as the optimum way to keep your teeth healthy and clean, but in reality simple, natural ingredients can be just as good for daily toothcare. Today's dental products are often found with unpleasant chemicals and synthetic additives which make their way into our bodies as we put them in our mouths, and into our waterways as they are washed down the sink. Most healthcare or dental products are also commonly found in very tough to recycle packaging, not unlike that found in the food industry.

We'll go through some widely used alternatives for toothcare in this chapter, but it is recommended that you consult your dentist on what he or she thinks is best for your current needs. Everyone has different dental requirements, so it doesn't hurt to ask before using these alternatives. There are also a variety of homemade recipes on the internet, so consider browsing a few alternatives if these recipes don't work for you.

Brushing and flossing

When it comes to taking care of a healthy smile, switching from a disposable plastic toothbrush to a natural toothbrush is a great first step. 5 billion plastic toothbrushes are made each year, often ending up in our landfills, ocean, or as litter. Bamboo is the most common environmentally conscious material available for toothbrushes today; it is one of the most sustainable fibres in the world, with the ability to grow to full height in just a few years without the use of synthetic fertilizers and pesticides. It is also water efficient, has natural anti-bacterial properties, and removes carbon dioxide from the air four times faster than trees.

Once your bamboo toothbrush is no longer usable, you can expand its life by using it as a cleaning tool to scrub small areas, or as a plant label in your garden. To compost the handle, pluck out the bristles from the handle with a pair of pliers. Whereas a plastic toothbrush will never truly degrade at the end of its life, bamboo toothbrush handles can be easily composted and the bristles recycled (be sure to check with your local authority, as these small plastic bristles are very light and can easily be lost.

No toothcare routine is complete without floss. Keeping your gums healthy can be done by opting for natural floss. Silk floss exists today as a compostable option, as regular floss is lined or made with plastic, and often comes packaged in plastic. You may also be able to find silk floss packaged in recyclable glass and metal packaging with the option to refill.

Make Your Own: Toothpaste

Toothpaste is often filled with synthetic ingredients such as propylene glycol (an active smoothing agent found in anti-freeze) and triclosan (a toxic, chlorinated ingredient with many health concerns such as slowing blood circulation). These ingredients travel not only into your own body, but also through waterways after going through the drain – not an ideal situation all-round. Luckily, a toothpaste alternative can be made with coconut oil, baking soda, and xylitol.

Baking soda works to clean the teeth and also helps to balance the mouth's pH levels for healthy bacteria, but can feel abrasive and harsh on its own, so adding additional ingredients such as xylitol and coconut oil helps to balance out the potential sensitivity. Xylitol is a natural ingredient derived from vegetables such as corn, and is already used by the dental industry in chewing gums and toothpaste. It acts as a sweetener, and also reduces the risk of cavities. It can be found at any good health or grocery shop. Coconut oil also has the ability to fight strains of bacteria that can lead to gum disease and tooth decay.

Materials

– Small, dry, clean jar with sealable lid
– 2 tablespoons coconut oil
– 1 tablespoon baking soda
– 1 tablespoon xylitol
– Few drops of peppermint essential oil (optional)

Method

Take your small jar and ensure that it is dry. Add 2 tablespoons of coconut oil, 1 tablespoon baking soda, and 1 tablespoon xylitol [1–3]. If the coconut oil is a bit too firm, you can soften it by putting it in the microwave for a few seconds. Mix these ingredients together until well combined. You can also add a few drops of peppermint essential oil for a minty flavour – start with 4 drops, and then add more to taste [4].

To use, take a small spoon and scoop out a pea-sized amount of toothpaste [5]. Brush as normal, but without the fear of chemical additives going into your mouth and down the drain!

It's best to make small amounts of this toothpaste at a time, to avoid any excess contamination and to keep it as fresh as possible.

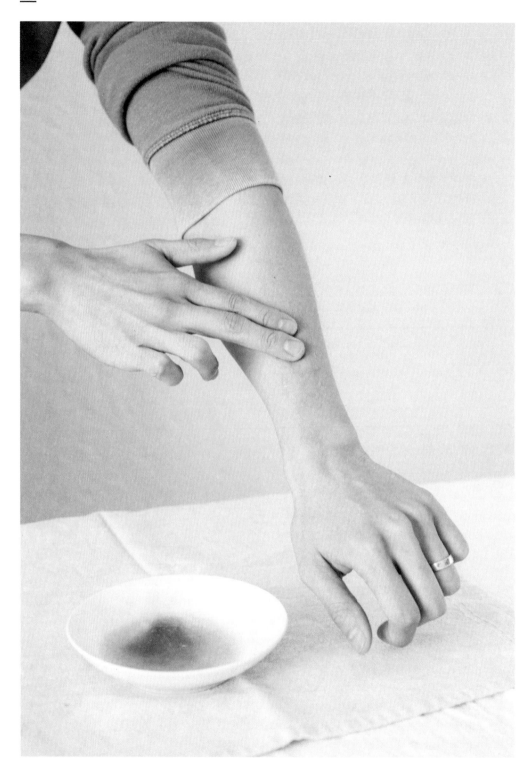

Body care

—

Body care products are commonly manufactured with large numbers of chemicals and artificial fragrances. Our skin is the largest organ on our body and it very easily soaks up the products we put on it – synthetic ingredients included. Wastewater treatment centres are unable to break down these ingredients when they are washed down our plugholes, and so they are also released into the ecosystem. Phthalates, silicones, or triclosan are some of the known chemicals in our soaps, lotions and sunscreens that emit harmful chemicals into the tissues of aquatic wildlife, ultimately disturbing the balance of our ocean's ecosystem.

Recently, the USA, Canada and the UK have banned the production of body cleansers containing plastic microbeads. While these small microbeads claim to help consumers exfoliate dead skin, they do not dissolve after they are rinsed off. Their small size makes it easy for them to flow into waterways, and very often they are mistaken for food by marine animals. This has potentially devastating consequences; the beads are adept at absorbing pollutants in the water, and can become up to a million times more toxic than the water around it. If you eat seafood, you may very well be ingesting plastic yourself without knowing it.

Keeping your body clean and cared for is as simple as starting off with a natural, organically-derived soap. Bar soap is easy to find locally made, and can often be found free of packaging, or with a recyclable paper wrapper instead of plastic. If you're looking for something more moisturizing, keep an eye out for ingredients such as shea butter or coconut oil. We'll explore a few homemade recipes as well in this chapter, as there are a variety of ways to incorporate natural, commonly found ingredients in to your body care routine.

Before diving into your next DIY project, also consider supporting small, local businesses creating eco-friendly body care products – some companies are offering refill programmes to help save on packaging waste, and are opting for more natural, eco-friendly ingredients. It might be more carbon and waste efficient to opt for a local producer that may be making products in bulk, rather than buying several small bottles or packages of ingredients for yourself. However, making DIY body care products can empower you to better understand what you are using, give you greater control over what goes into your products, and be a fun project to do at home.

Make Your Own: Aloe Vera Gel and Scrub

Aloe vera is well known for its beneficial qualities – amongst many things, it has been known to strengthen the immune system, reduce arthritis pain, cure dermatitis, alleviate menstrual aches and heal wounds. It has also been proven to lower cholesterol, prevent diabetes and assuage muscle pain – a real wonder plant!

Part of the succulent family, it grows best in warm, dry climates, which makes it the perfect house plant. Within those thick leaves is a gel which provides the perfect base for skincare products. There are many active compounds, minerals, and antioxidants in aloe vera gel which can treat your skin. In fact, you'll often see it listed as an ingredient in mass-produced cosmetic products. Below is a wonderfully simple recipe which can be used as a moisturiser, as well as a body scrub.

Materials
– Sharp knife
– Cutting board
– 1 aloe leaf
– Blender
– Handful of cane sugar or sea salt

Method
Take a sharp knife and cut a leaf from the base of your aloe plant. Rinse the leaf and then carefully cut away the pointed edges [1].

Next, cut off one of the sides of the aloe leaf, so you can clearly see all the slimy, water-filled tissue within [2].

With a spoon, scoop out all the tissue from the leaf [3]. Put the tissue into a blender, and blend until smooth and no longer clumpy [4]. The blended tissue may appear foamy at first, but the foam will disappear [5].

If keeping the aloe as a moisturiser, store for a few days in a sealed container in the fridge. Apply to burns or dry patches to alleviate your skin from pain or irritation.

If using as a scrub, mix in the handful of cane sugar or sea salt [6]. Use as either a face or body scrub.

Make Your Own: Body Butter

Natural body butter can be made with just a few ingredients: shea butter, cocoa butter, and coconut oil are great options with antioxidants and fatty acids that can soften the skin. If you enjoy the smell of cocoa butter, you can opt out of adding a few drops of essential oil.

Note that this recipe will react differently in different climates – depending on where you live, these ingredients may not remain in their solid state at room temperature, or may become too hard. Feel free to alter the recipe by adding more solid oils for a warmer climate, or adding more liquid oils such as sweet almond oil and olive oil for cooler climates.

Materials
– 28 g (1 oz) shea butter
– 28 g (1 oz) cocoa butter
– 28 g (1 oz) coconut oil
– Glass or metal bowl
– Small saucepan
– Essential oil (optional)
– Handheld mixer – with whisk attachment
– Dry, clean jar with sealable lid

Method
For this recipe, place equal parts shea butter, cocoa butter, and coconut oil into a glass or metal bowl [1–3].

Create a double boiler by simmering a small volume of water in a pan underneath the bowl containing your butters and oils [4]. Allow the double boiler to melt the oils in the bowl – be careful, this will be hot. Feel free to add a few drops of your favourite essential oil to scent your body butter.

Once melted and combined, allow the oils to cool in the freezer or fridge until almost completely solidified. Using a hand held mixer, whip up the solidified oils until nice and creamy. Use a spatula to scoop all the body butter up into a clean jar for storage – make sure it is leak-proof in case your body butter starts to melt on a warmer day [5].

Make Your Own: Lip Balm

Coconut oil and cocoa butter can also make a simple lip balm. The fatty acids of these oils keep your lips moisturized throughout the day. If you live in a warmer climate, adding beeswax can help keep your lip balm solidified.

Materials
– 1 tablespoon coconut oil
– 1 tablespoon cocoa butter
– Glass or metal bowl
– Small saucepan
– Dry, clean jar with sealable lid

Method
Place 1 tablespoon of coconut oil and 1 tablespoon of cocoa butter in a glass or metal bowl [1–2].

Create a double boiler by simmering a small volume of water in a saucepan underneath the bowl containing your butters and oils. Allow the double boiler to melt the oils in the bowl – be careful, this will be hot [3].

Once melted, pour the oils into a leak-proof container – a small metal tin once used for lip balm works, or reuse a miniature honey or jam jar [4].

Allow the oil to cool in the fridge or at room temperature. Once solidified, the balm is ready to use [5–6].

Haircare

—

Radiant, smooth and shining locks of hair cover countless magazines and commercials on the television, all of which claim that a particular hair product will turn your hair into a spectacle sure to turn every head in the room. Long gone are the simple shampoos used previously – today's hair regimen consists of hair serums, oils, tools and multiple chemical processes. These products though, as well as certain hair treatments, can add up in costs both financial and environmental.

Why not flaunt your natural locks instead of altering them in a way society deems fit? Embrace your natural texture and colour. Although it's often exciting to get a new colour or style, there are still ways to have fun without sacrificing the health of your hair and the environment. Whether it's getting a different hair cut or trying natural dyes such as henna to lighten your hair, consider looking into more natural alternatives for the sake of your scalp and the planet.

The principles for sustainable hair care are the same as those for body care – opting for natural ingredients to avoid causing harm to the ecosystems they will eventually end up in is critical to ensuring the balance of ocean ecosystems for generations to come. Sulphates, propylene glycol, and parabens are some commonly found chemicals that act as preservatives or foaming ingredients, yet these ingredients can actually strip your hair of the nutrients it needs and irritate your skin. The dyes commonly used to colour hair are also made with thousands of chemicals, and some of these chemicals are known to cause cancer in animals, so potentially humans as well.

Most of us have a daily routine that involves cleaning or removing our hair. We'll explore some sustainable practices for this, but also explore how our hair accessories and beauty tools can provide areas of opportunity.

Shampoo and shampoo bars

Look for shampoos that are devoid of unnatural chemicals and preservatives. Several companies now exist that sell shampoo made from naturally-derived ingredients. Keep an eye out for bulk purchase stores also, where you can bring your own containers to refill with your chosen shampoo over and over, significantly reducing your plastic intake.

Shampoo bars are a great alternative to traditional packaged shampoo, and make for easy travelling also. You can purchase them without packaging or often in recyclable paper packaging. These bars work similarly to soap, and lather up when wet with water. Simply rub the bar into your hands and scrub through your hair, just as you would with regular shampoo.

If your hair is naturally quite dry, consider using coconut oil and a bit of honey as a deep conditioner and strengthening formula, rather than chemical-heavy in-shower conditioners. Apply the oil to your hair and scalp before showering, and let it sit for twenty minutes before rinsing off. Coconut oil has been proven to help reduce keratin loss in your hair, while honey retains moisture.

All in all, think critically about how often your hair needs to be washed – every single day isn't always necessary, especially when some shampoos can strip your hair of nutrients. In time, training your scalp to produce less oils by washing your hair less will mean less shampoo is needed, and more water conserved.

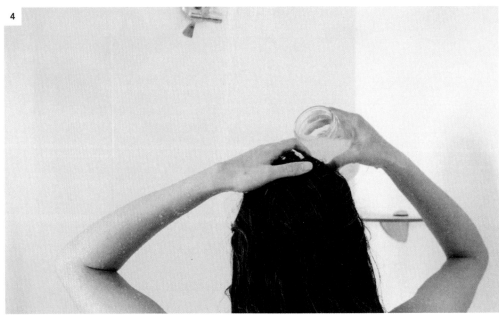

Make Your Own: Apple Cider Rinse

Depending on your local water source, shampoo bars may be difficult to rinse out compared to conventional shampoo due to hard water (water with high mineral content). This could leave your hair feeling grimy as the minerals cling onto your hair. To fix this, use an apple cider vinegar rinse for your hair to remove unnecessary residue on your hair.

Ingredients

– 1 tablespoon apple cider vinegar
– Jar or cup
– 250ml (8½ fl oz) water
– Essential oil of your choice

Method

Pour 1 tablespoon of apple cider vinegar into a jar or cup that can hold 250ml of water [1–2]. To get rid of the harsh vinegar smell, add a few drops of an essential oil of your choosing.

After wetting your hair in the shower, fill the container with water [3]. Slowly pour over wet hair, and scrub through your scalp [4]. Rinse your hair with the entire mixture, and wash until all the vinegar residue is removed.

After washing

After washing, I recommend letting your hair dry naturally. Hair dryers use quite a bit of energy and concentrated heat to dry your hair. When possible, use sparingly in order to reduce your electricity usage, and also keep your hair free of heat treatment (which can easily damage your hair). Instead, use an absorbent towel, shake out water which is concentrated at the roots of your scalp, or allow it to dry in the sun.

If your hair becomes frizzy after drying, using a bit of coconut oil or other natural oil can help tame small hairs – note that these oils can be very effective, so use only a little at a time.

For hair styling, natural wood combs, hair brushes and accessories also exist which can be composted at end of use unlike their plastic counterparts. A natural hair stick can be used to put your hair into an updo, or you can look for naturally derived hair-ties to tie up hair (made from compostable natural rubber and cotton). If you are looking for some new hair accessories to change up your look, consider finding sustainable brands and small artisans making their own accessories – the availability of natural, organic options such as bamboo is on the rise.

Safety razor

It is estimated that 2 billion disposable razors are thrown away on an annual basis. Similar to plastic toothbrushes, plastic razors are made to be used for only a limited period of time, but last for thousands of years in landfill. Although plastic razors can be a cheap one-time purchase, the costs add up. It's wiser, financially and sustainably, to opt for a longer-lasting metal safety razor.

Metal safety razors may appear a bit intimidating at first, but are designed to help angle the razor for the safest yet closest shave. These razors were once popular back in the late 1800s – before plastic disposables became more prominent – and are made entirely from metal, with recyclable razor blades. Check with the company you purchased the razor from, to see if the blades can be recycled by them, or if they can be recycled locally.

Safety razors can be used with simple bar soap as a substitute for shaving cream, which is usually found in non-recyclable packaging, or some brands sell shaving brushes which can lather up soap for a smooth application. A shaving brush can also lightly exfoliate skin and release any trapped hairs.

Each safety razor may have a different mechanism to open, but it is fairly easy to replace the blades by opening the top of the razor. Turning the handle of the razor usually allows the top to loosen in order for the blade to come out. Be careful when handling the blades for replacement.

When shaving, make sure that your skin is moisturized and lathered with soap to ensure a closer and smoother shave. Shaving during or after a shower makes for an easier process, as hair softens when wet. Allow the weight of the razor to guide your hand as it pulls along your skin, and slowly pull the razor across your skin. Use your hand to gently pull the razor, being careful not to apply force. The blades of a safety razor are designed in a way so that their placement makes for the safest shave for your skin.

In between strokes, flip the razor to the opposite side of the blade for a cleaner shave, as hair will get stuck inside the blade. Rinse the razor to dislodge stray hairs as you go. When done, lightly pat the razor with a dry towel and leave in the open air to allow it to dry.

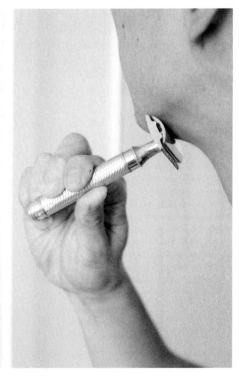

Water usage

—

Water is a finite resource used by everyone in the world: by 2025, it is estimated that two thirds of the world's population will experience water stress. Only 1 per cent of our world's water is fresh, and it's becoming limited year after year due to climate change, which is drying up the lakes and rivers that we once depended on. Droughts are becoming more common as temperatures continue to rise, so several cities have mandated lowering the usage of water in residents' homes in order to salvage the water supply.

Water is used everywhere, from the forests harvested for furniture to the farmlands that grow our crops. Households also use water in their gardens, and need it to clean and cook in the home. There is no denying that water is a valuable resource that is needed in almost every single industry and facet of life, and our bodies also rely heavily on clean drinking water in order to survive.

In the bathroom, we also use water to cleanse and relieve ourselves. The toilet, sink, and shower are the main sources of water – when not properly monitored or if taken for granted, we can easily waste quite a bit of water on a daily basis. This not only puts stress on water sources in your local environment, but can also put a dent in your wallet. For water-scarce communities, water prices may be much higher due to low supply.

This chapter will focus specifically on what you can do for your shower and toilet, as they are the primary sources of water usage in the bathroom. I've personally applied some of these small tricks to reduce my water usage, and have found it rather easy to implement. Saving water doesn't have to be difficult, and only needs a bit of thought and attention when in use.

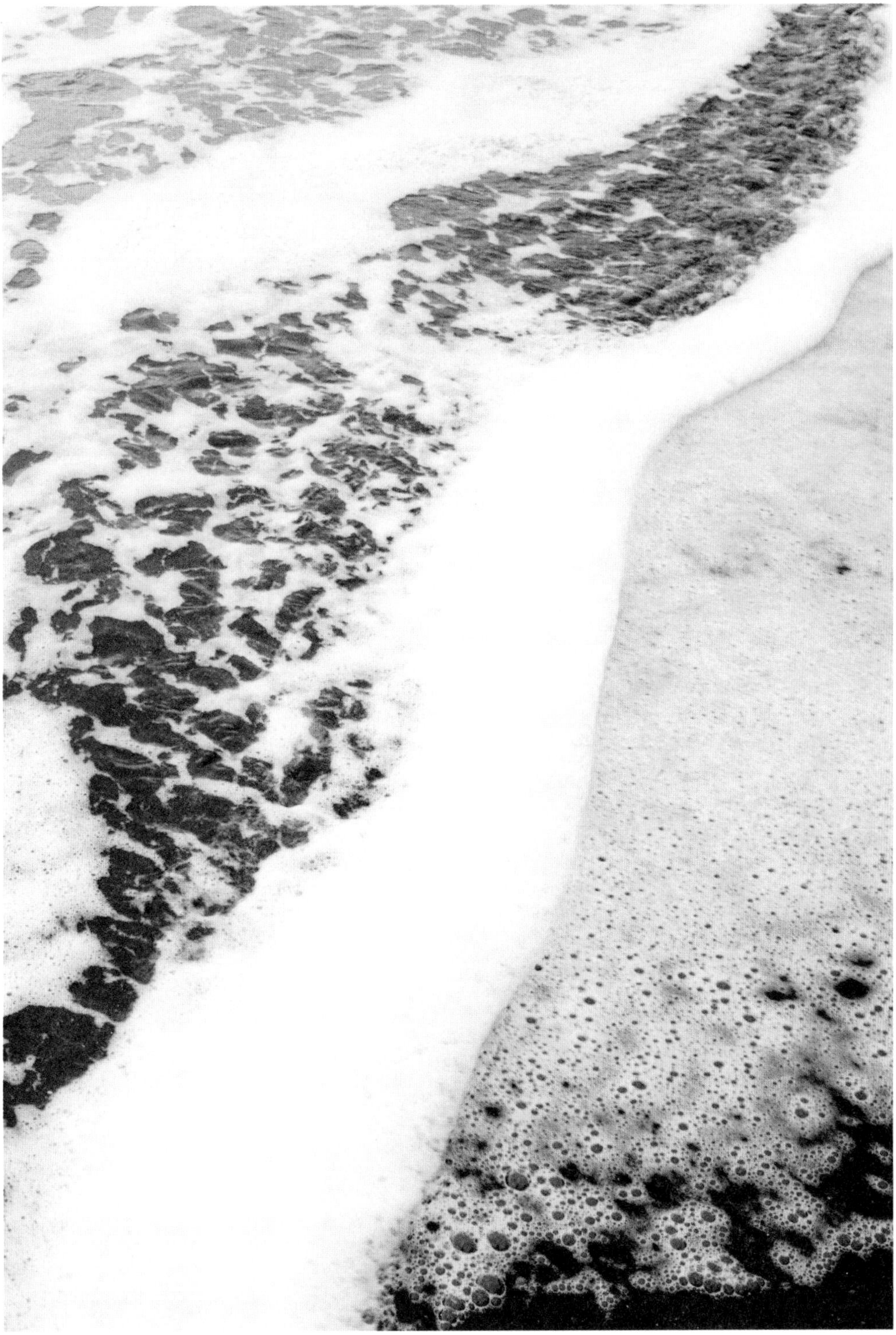

Shower

70 per cent of our water usage today occurs within the home – the shower is one of the top three sources of water use. In order to save water in the shower, a few simple steps can be done right away.

– Reduce shower times to 5 minutes or less and turn off water while shampooing or soaping your body.
– If it takes a long time for water to heat up, consider fixing your water heater to decrease the amount of water wasted, or keep a bucket in the shower to collect the excess water for watering the garden. Better yet, try a cold shower in the morning. The energy used to heat the water is saved, and the burst of fresh cool will keep your skin moisturized – it makes for a pretty invigorating start to the day too!

– Installing a low-flow shower head can also help reduce your water consumption. A conventional shower head will use 3–4 gallons of water per minute, whereas modern low-flow shower heads can reduce consumption to 1–2 gallons per minute. In water sensitive areas, this can also save households plenty of money due to high water costs.

Keep in mind that water is a precious commodity. Every time you step into the shower or turn on the tap, keep the water on a low flow, and turn off the water when it isn't needed – sometimes it's easy to forget how much water is lost when brushing your teeth or washing your face. Be sure to fix any leaks right away (the average home attributes 12 per cent of water use to leaks).

Toilet

Similar to the shower, the toilet is a prime opportunity for saving water in the home. For a short term solution, using a weight to displace water in the cistern is a simple way to reduce the amount of water used to flush the toilet.

To do this, you can use an old plastic bottle filled with sand and water, or any weight that will not touch the toilet's moving parts. Some hardware stores also sell used bricks – a very affordable water displacement option.

Simply remove the cover from the top of the cistern and submerge the weight in the tank. You will notice that the level of water will rise as you put the weight in. By placing the weight into the tank, you will reduce the amount of water required to fill the cistern (which you'll find is often more than enough). You may need to play around with different size weights to ensure that your toilet is still getting enough water pressure to be able to flush though. Put the cover back on the toilet tank, and you're good to go.

If it's time for a toilet replacement, opt for dual-flush toilets that use different amounts of water for solid versus liquid waste. Remember that there's no need to buy a completely new toilet unless it's broken beyond repair and you truly need a replacement – consider the emissions and resources needed to extract the materials and manufacture a new toilet. You're far better off with sticking to the old toilet and seeing what you can do to help conserve water with what you already have.

Toilet paper is another hot topic when it comes to bathroom waste – the average North American supposedly uses 57 sheets of toilet paper a day, generating about 165 lbs of CO_2 emissions generated per year. 437 billion gallons of water, 253,000 tons of bleach, and 15 million trees are used annually in America alone for the production of toilet paper.

One roll of virgin paper amounts to 730 grams of CO_2 emissions, but a recycled toilet paper roll uses half the emissions. Bamboo toilet paper is also a great alternative, as we know of bamboo's many sustainability benefits. Look for toilet paper wrapped in paper as well, or for sustainable toilet paper brands that are consciously producing their products with minimal environmental impact.

It is also rather inexpensive to install a bidet. Bidets help reduce potential infections and diseases as well, more-so than toilet paper. While a towel or a bit of toilet paper may still be needed, the impact of using a bit of water is noticeable – 90 per cent of the toilet paper that would otherwise be used is saved when using a bidet.

Cleaning materials

—

Your bathroom can quite quickly build up with dirt and grime. As with other areas of the home that are prone to spillages and stains, such as the kitchen, it is necessary to clean the space regularly in order to prevent the build up of bacteria and the growth of mould. Cleaning countertops, mirrors, the toilet and shower, however, is often undertaken with the help of cleaning products that are packed full of harmful chemicals (the better for killing bacteria and creating shine).

Common ingredients in commercial cleaning products can be toxic – their fumes can irritate the eyes, skin, and respiratory system. These chemicals are also difficult to handle and dispose of, which poses a threat to aquatic wildlife and overall water quality. For example, alkylphenol ethoxylates are known to be a endocrine disrupter, as they cause adverse reproductive effects in wildlife. The lengthy, alien names of chemical ingredients listed on the back of many chemical cleaners are baffling to the majority of us, making it difficult to understand what's in them.

The companies producing these chemical-heavy materials currently do not have clear industry certifications to measure the safety and sustainability of their products. Though some organizations exist online to help rate and score the safety of modern day body care and cleaning products, companies still have some work to do by way of explaining the purpose of each ingredient and consequently providing transparency for the consumer.

In the meantime, we'll look into some natural and safe options to clean your space, which could also save you money. Common household ingredients used in food recipes can also be used for cleaning, and are as effective as their unhealthy counterparts – sometimes even more effective. Consider using some of the following alternatives to clean your bathroom, as well as the other rooms in your home.

Natural cleaning products

Cleaning your home can be done simply and sustainably with just a few natural ingredients. The following can be bought at a fraction of the price of commercial cleaning products and, when combined, make for great cleaning tools to be used throughout the home.

— White vinegar or apple cider vinegar are great anti-microbial cleaners. They can usually be found in bulk containers, or can be purchased in a large plastic jug.
— Lemons are fantastic for cleaning in a multitude of ways. They're great at killing unwanted bacteria due to their acidity. They can also help remove odours left on containers, chopping boards and utensils – just give them a good rub-down with half a lemon before washing.

— Baking soda is another affordable cleaning ingredient that is abundantly found in North America, mined from trona mineral deposits, and usually sitting in your kitchen cupboard. Besides being commonly used for baking yummy desserts, it can also be utilized as a deodorizer, scouring agent for hard to clean spots, and more. By simply adding a bit of water to baking soda, the paste can be used to clean stained spots on the bathtub, sink, and counter – it can even be used to clean your toilet!
— Castile soap is a simple vegetable based soap made from oil, water, and lye. It is also biodegradable, which makes it great for marine ecosystems. Castile soap should not be mixed with any acidic ingredients like vinegar, as the ingredients will cancel out

each other's effectiveness. It often comes in uplifting, fresh scents such as tea tree or citrus. It can be used to clean surfaces, wash dishes, and more.

– Essential oils are made from a high concentration of plant extracts. Ranging from scents such as lavender and tea tree to grapefruit, these oils are a great alternative to synthetic perfumes, and can be added to your natural cleaning agents to help freshen the home. Be sure to find sustainably-minded essential oil brands, as it takes large quantities of plant matter to make these oils in their concentrated forms.

Use these natural cleaning solutions with an upcycled rag from an old t-shirt or with natural scrubbers. Loofahs made from dehydrated gourd are quite popular in Asian countries, and are easily cut into multiple sponges for your body or for cleaning. Other hand-held wooden natural scrubbers or plant-based sponges can also take the place of traditional plastic sponges which degrade over time, releasing small plastic particles into the ocean.

Make Your Own: Cleaning Spray

A simple cleaning spray can be made with water, vinegar, and essential oil (if you'd like to add a scent). Use this all-purpose cleaning spray to wipe down dirty counters, kill bacteria, scrub the toilet, and clean windows or glass. Repurpose an old spray bottle package from a previously used product, or there are plenty of glass bottle options available for purchase online.

Ingredients

– 150 ml (5 fl oz) water
– 150 ml (5 fl oz) vinegar
– Spray bottle
– Essential oil of your choice

Method

Measure out your water and vinegar. Pour both of these ingredients into a spray bottle of your choice [1–2].

Add a few drops of essential oil to the water if you like, to help balance the harsh smell of vinegar.

This spray can be used to sanitize mirrors, clean windows, and eliminate bacteria in the nooks and crannies of your bathtub or countertop [3]. It's also a great alternative for cleaning the toilet, as vinegar kills bacteria and mould.

1

2

3

Outdoors

As discussed in the introduction to this book, the home is the perfect place to start on your journey to living a more eco-friendly lifestyle. We are often very emotionally attached to the personal spaces we cultivate with family and friends, and so it makes sense to start here when caring for the environment.

However, the outdoors presents a host of opportunities to drive sustainable change in the same way. We step outside to go to work, travel, socialize and more, and in each of these areas there are myriad ways to make the associated activities more environmentally friendly, and your carbon footprint much lighter.

Going through the experience of making your own home more sustainable can train your mind towards thinking more sustainably about everything you do – it's important to take this attitude beyond the four walls of your house. Though it may start as a personal journey, it is more than likely that you'll encounter people and situations that offer opportunities for improvement. It is these opportunities that will give you the chance to speak up and make change for the people and community around you. Sustainability doesn't have to end at the front door; step outside and remain mindful of how your everyday choices impact the planet you live on.

Greening the workplace
—

Outside of the home, many of us spend a good part of our weekdays working full or part-time in order to sustain ourselves financially. Your personal everyday work routine can be adapted in various ways to improve your ecological credentials, but there may also be opportunities to work with the team around you and spread awareness along the way. The following principles should serve as a guide to leading a more environmentally friendly working life, but they can also be applied if you are a student at university, college, or even at school – there's no age limit when it comes to driving change!

On a personal level, look to reduce your waste and energy footprint wherever you go. Choose reusables over single use items at the workplace cafeteria, or bring your own meal with all reusable lunchware. Opt to print on recycled paper, or use a digital copy if possible. If you're using a computer, turn it off at the end of the day, unplugging devices when possible to reduce any potential electricity usage. Turn off conference room lights when not in use and power off projectors as well.

Once you notice things in the office that are beyond your own personal control, you may be inclined to go above and beyond in changing your company's everyday operations, but you'll need a few more hands by your side. In light of this, many corporations today have self-organized 'green teams' which are dedicated to greening the office space. Green team employees volunteer any extra time they have outside of their full time job to help make changes to their offices. Some potential campaign ideas include:

- Reducing disposable cup use in the office
- Working to promote responsible pension plan investment for employees
- Providing meatless, plant based meals in the cafeteria
- Running a company garden
- Providing on-site composting

If your company doesn't already have any green advocates making changes in the office, consider finding a few more like-minded coworkers that may want to help you. Though it may take time, courage and effort to start a group on your own, it is much easier to drive change with a team and is well worth the experience. You'll not only be changing the planet, but will hopefully form wonderful relationships along the way.

Campaigns like this are most successful when they seek to understand their company environment. Mapping out the problem you'd like to solve, and understanding your stakeholders' opinions, goals or potential pushbacks are extremely important to drive any company change. In addition, if there are any potential company leaders that can sponsor you efforts, or partnerships that can be made, consider building those relationships to maximize your overall impact. Some of the groups you may want to contact or be aware of are your company's sustainability team (to determine if they have any goals you can align to, otherwise they are great subject-matter experts), facilities management, and employee engagement. Of course, be sure to always be connected to the employees affected, and be sure to have an open ear and mind to gather feedback for improvement on how changes can be better implemented.

Dining out

—

Dining out is becoming more and more popular in the modern age, but when you aren't preparing and serving your food yourself, it can be difficult to keep tabs on the sustainable nature of your eating.

In the case of takeaways, it's highly likely that your dinner will come with a pile of one time use plastic utensils, non recyclable plastic boxes, and perhaps some condiment packets and napkins, all bagged up and tied together in a convenient plastic bag. As our society moves faster and more efficiently than ever before, there is a push for convenient and quick meal options which are often served in single use containers. Opting to visit a restaurant and dine in rather than ordering is more environmentally friendly – most restaurants use reusable plates, cups and forks, although even in some sit down restaurants there will be times you will be offered disposable items instead of reusable.

So when dining out, whether picking up a coffee and breakfast to go in the morning or grabbing a Chinese takeaway to have at home, consider bringing some of the following to help reduce your plastic waste:

1. A reusable bottle or cup for drinks. Remind your server that you don't need a plastic cup since you already have your own!
2. A set of reusable utensils from your home – if metal ones are too cumbersome, consider purchasing a lightweight bamboo set of cutlery. Again, remind whoever is packing up your food that you do not need a set of plastic utensils. Make sure to check before you leave – if they happen to pop some in, you can politely ask them to take them back.
3. A reusable stainless steel straw for your drink. When a waiter asks what you'd like to drink, ask for the drink with no straw, and show them that you already have a straw to reinforce the request. In the US alone, 500 million straws are used everyday, and because of their lightweight nature, are notorious as a harmful source of plastic pollution. Single use plastic straws are also not typically recycled. So opt for reusable straws – they also come in various diameters – paired with a reusable cup for your next smoothie or boba tea. You can also get bamboo or glass straws.
4. A reusable napkin to substitute for one-time use paper napkins. Bleached paper is an energy and water intensive process so I look to reduce paper usage whenever possible. You can show your waiter that you already brought your own napkin and politely ask them to take back your unused napkins. Also remind restaurant employees, if they are preparing your food for takeaway, that they do not need to include a heap of disposable napkins.
5. Stainless steel containers are also great for packing up leftovers, instead of getting another one-time-use container that will be tossed later on. You can use tupperware if you have any as well. If you're getting a takeaway, calling a restaurant beforehand and asking if they will allow you to bring in your own reusable container is also a great option. Checking restaurant reviews and photos from previous customers online can give you a better sense of what type of container you might need to fit the amount of food they serve, or else, a larger container is a safer bet.

Going places

—

Though energy consumption is one of the largest sources of emissions from our homes, global transportation accounts for 14 per cent of total greenhouse gas emissions today. The majority of vehicles are still powered with nonrenewable fossil fuels which emit CO_2 and other greenhouse gases into the atmosphere, thus contributing to climate change. Yet transportation isn't going away anytime soon, since we have to get from place to place – whether it's for work or running errands. Instead, we can strive for minimal impact, only travelling abroad when truly necessary, and better understand the impact of each mode of transport to help make a more educated decision.

Of all modes of transportation for an individual, the aeroplane generates the most greenhouse gases per trip. When lined up in order of impact, a flight produces ten times more emissions compared to a bicycle ride of the same distance, whereas a small, efficient car is six times worse, with trains and buses following after. However, we all understand how tempting it is to hop on a plane to experience a different country – studies show that today's generation is traveling more than any other, due to the appeal of exploring new places and the fairly newfound affordability of flights. So if you would like to travel abroad, consider a few things such as a similar experience closer to where you live. Flying can still be an option, but flying less often will make those trips overseas all the more special.

For local trips, remember that walking and cycling produce the least emissions. If something is a safe walking or biking distance from where you are, consider getting a few steps or pedals in for your health and for your planet. Of course, these are not always an option, so your next best bet is to find public transportation options. Consider taking a train or bus to your next vacation hotspot to cut at least two-thirds of your carbon emissions.

Owning a car also has the added bonus of increased independence. Purchase your own vehicles sparingly though, especially if your local community has a selection of public transportation links, or has great walking and biking routes. Electric and hybrid vehicles are the cleaner options for cars, although these vehicles still need charging, often by dirty, emission-producing energy sources. Such vehicles also run on batteries that contain toxic chemicals that are difficult to dispose of. Make sure to carry out plenty of research when deciding to buy a vehicle, determining how it will be powered, its efficiency, etc. Consider buying used also, as this will offset the manufacturing emissions of a new car.

If you happen to own a car already, your car's fuel efficiency can change depending on how you drive it. Decelerating and accelerating at a milder pace can help reduce the amount of fuel needed. Driving 10 mph slower – or at least adhering to the speed limit, as we ought to – is also more fuel efficient. Of course, choose to carpool when you can also, as this maximizes the use of both vehicle and fuel.

Take action

—

Getting out into your local community is one of the best ways to drive change for a better world. Below are a few ideas to help you get started.

Picking up litter

Every year, 9 billion tons of litter end up in our oceans, posing a threat to marine life. Even on land, various animals can be tricked into thinking plastic waste is food, and various chemicals in our products can leach into our fresh water systems. It doesn't take much to pick up litter in your local community – you can do it with a group of friends, strangers or on your own. On your next outdoor hike or walk, bring something to store litter in as you go. A lightweight paper bag that can be later composted, or a sturdier bucket which can be washed are some great options. If you aren't too fond of handling litter with your bare hands, you can look for compostable rubber gloves or purchase a tool to help grab dirty waste.

Be sure to separate recyclable items when possible so they can be properly recycled by your municipality. Roughly rinsing the items before recycling will increase the likelihood of the items being recycled – many recycling companies will need to pay extra for washing items so doing a quick rinse on your part definitely helps.

Speak up and vote

There is no better way to influence change than by governmental voting. Exercising your political right to support various causes in your community is an important privilege and right everyone should be aware of. The more we care about the state of the planet, the more we ought to go out and make sure our governing officials know how to lead our communities and countries towards a better future.

Today's businesses are also learning to be more customer-centric. Take a few minutes to send a quick message to a local business or brand. If possible, offer a specific action or solution to help drive sustainable change. It could be asking the company for more environmentally friendly packaging, or inquiring as to whether they manufacture and operate their company with renewable energy. The more we speak up, the more aware these companies will become that sustainable business practices are a critical purchasing decision factor today, and for generations to come.

Donate time or resources

Working with organizations that are already looking to create a more sustainable world is an effective way to volunteer your time. Your local government may already have an environmental sustainability education programme rolled out in local schools that could use a few extra volunteers, or an environmental nonprofit with a meaningful mission could always use your help.

People willing to invest their time and care encourage such entities to continue with their efforts. If you're a busy bee and have a packed schedule, consider donating anything the organization needs – extra gardening equipment for a local food co-op, monetary donations, etc. Look to equip and empower the organizations that are already doing great work in your area.

'The power of one man or one woman doing the right thing for the right reason, and at the right time, is the greatest influence in our society.'

Conclusion

—

Sustainability doesn't happen overnight. I've realized over the years that sustainability is a journey. As I took on conscious consumerism a few years back, minimalism a year later, and a zero waste lifestyle most recently, it became clear that the definition for sustainable living changes constantly – as our society looks for improved, innovative ways to sustain our planet. But I can say with full confidence, no matter what chapter of sustainable living I have been in, I have always thoroughly enjoyed and appreciated being able to live a life that tries its best to actively respond to the problems it creates.

I've been asked many times, "Christine, does it really matter if I make a change to live more sustainably? There's too many other people in the world, why do my actions really matter?" And in response, I think about my own life. I think about the lives of other sustainability bloggers, activists, and professionals. Do the changes in my life, and in their lives matter? To that I would have to say, "Absolutely."

I dove into sustainable living with one purpose: to do the right thing. However, I never would have thought that my lifestyle changes would impact people around me, enough to make them think differently, or perhaps even change… but they have. So to those of you who doubt that your actions matter, imagine if the whole world had that mentality – humankind would have never been able to master flight, create the internet, or reach the moon. If we all live in doubt and fear that our actions don't matter, we will fail to progress towards a better future.

Our world needs positive change more than ever amid the pressing issues of climate change and environmental degradation. Though this book is a primer on maintaining a more sustainable home, I hope you acknowledge that the small steps you may end up taking because of this book are a bold statement to the world that we can change the status quo. Yes, you are one individual out of more than 7 billion, but your actions matter and have the potential to positively change the lives and mindsets of the people around you.

Index

Acknowledgements

—

More than a year ago, I was approached with the idea of authoring a book and quite honestly, I didn't believe that I had what it takes. It was my closest peers who encouraged me to embark upon the massive task of writing *Sustainable Home*, and I am so grateful and humbled that they believed in me more than I believed in myself.

I would like to first thank my husband, Peter, who was my right hand, support, and encouragement throughout this journey. Because of you Peter, I was able to overcome my fear of failure. I would also like to thank my parents, sister, and brother-in-law for their support throughout the process, and for reminding me to always take care of myself first. Thanks also to Karen and Midori for being part of the photography process, my coworkers who mentored me, and my church family who prayed for me throughout. A special shout-out to Shia Su (Wasteland Rebel) and Kathryn Kellogg (Going Zero Waste) too, for being an instrumental part of my zero waste and blogging journey.

Above all, I thank God for the opportunity He has given me to share my passion through my blog, and now through this book.

First Published in 2018 by White Lion Publishing,
an imprint of The Quarto Group.
The Old Brewery, 6 Blundell Street,
London N7 9BH, United Kingdom.
T (0)20 7700 6700 F (0)20 7700 8066
www.QuartoKnows.com

A catalogue record for this book is available from
the British Library.

ISBN 978-0-7112-3969-2

2 3 4 5 6 7 8 9

Typeset in Avenir

Printed and bound in China